Outskirts

pp

Outskirts

Collected Poems

Jane Galer

pp

poiésis press

Mendocino   Menlo Park

Poiêsis Press
An imprint of Poiêsis Publishing Group
Mendocino, California
poiesispress.com

Printed in the United States.
22 21 20 19 18 17 16   1 2 3 4 5

Poems in Part 1 were previously published in Too Deep for Tears,
© 2007 by Jane Galer.
Poems in Part II were previously published in The Spirit Birds,
© 2012 by Jane Galer.

ISBN 978-0-9845697-9-3 (Softcover)
ISBN 978-0-9845697-5-5 (Hardcover)

Cover artwork: The Magic Circle, 1886, John William Waterhouse (1849-1917)
Cover photograph: ©Tate, London 2015.

About Poiêsis Press:
Poiêsis \'poi-ah-sis\ n. Greek; a creation, beginning, the root word for poetry, as in a bringing forth

We view the creative process as the complicity between the energies of muse and of mind. It is this commingling of energy that we think of as poiêsis. Poiêsis Press is dedicated to care-taking the energy of artistic creation, not feeding from it. We seek by what we publish to understand the complicated intercourse of word and art: the distillation of the creative urge into ink on paper.

Printed on acid free paper.

Also by Jane Galer

The Navigator's Wife

Becoming Hummingbird:
  Charting Your Life Journey the Shaman's Way

How I Learned to Smoke: An American Girl in Iran

The Spirit Birds

Too Deep for Tears

journal writing:

Piecework magazine

Coreopsis Journal of Myth and Theater

EarthLines: The Culture of Nature

In memory of my grandfather
Howard Myers Payne
(1895—1995)

*In your light I learn how to love. In your beauty, how to make poems.
You dance inside my chest where no one sees you, but sometimes I
do, and that sight becomes this art.*
—Rumi

Contents

Part 2 *The Spirit Birds*

Part 3 *New Poems*

Foreword

Some believe that the poem's most exalted form is the utterance of the alchemist or shaman: she who sees (in Shakespeare's words in *King Lear*), with Cordelia's washed eyes, the world beyond the world in which one lives and the magical connections between those realms.

I share this belief. Homer, Dante, Chaucer and Shakespeare accomplished this divine task. So did Rumi, Hafiz, W. B. Yeats, Virginia Woolf and Emily Dickinson, among others; in our time, certain poets join this company: Jane Hirshfield, Mary Oliver, Mark Jarman, W. S. Merwin, Maxine Kumin, Dennis Sampson, to name a significant few. The publication of Jane Galer's *Collected Poems* confirms her presence among these luminaries.

She takes her place in this company as, in fact, its only true shaman. Trained and certified in the shamanic arts in Peru, Galer is a sought after mentor and spirit guide as well as a stellar poet. But as I've said, the two roles are complimentary; they go hand in hand. The shaman who extends her practice inevitably ventures into the realm of poetry; the poet who hungers for knowledge and expression that dives deeper than the temporal will evolve into spiritual teaching and storytelling. Jane Galer found her way into both roles, rather like the earnest caterpillar that digests itself and morphs into a butterfly. The transformation is edgy and miraculous, and that's how one feels reading the poems here from Galer's previous collections, *Too Deep for Tears* and *Spirit Birds*, and 93 new and previously unpublished poems.

From the beginning more than two decades ago, Galer's poems have surged and shoaled on the page, and in the ear, with relentless curiosity about the way that words can be combined to evoke what may be thought of as unsayable. Here you will find accomplished sonnets, haiku and elegy, as well as other formal patterns that are modified to reveal new possibilities. Often, the poems feel like chants and incantations; often, that is just what they are.

Galer's poetry also restlessly and relentlessly strives after more than stylistic equanimity. One might say this is true of all poems, yet so few truly achieve it. These poems do so over and over again. I suspect they do because this poet understands, intuitively and intellectually, that the only balance worth achieving is between the natural and what one may accurately call (for our time and place) the domestic world; one might also refer to these as inner and outer worlds. Galer's poems are constantly playing back and forth on the taut chords that connect these domains. The music they make resonates; it rings true. Here are lines from the poem, *Wild Wind*, which evoke the shaman's calling as mentor, respect for nature, and the human need for communication:

> I can teach you how dark the wild wind is.
> Sling together worlds of gods in likenesses
> Indescribable desired by the likes of you and me.

This way of seeing and expressing is formal and relaxed in the same way that a mountain meadow and a family reunion achieve memorable balance. All the elements, high and low, are granted equal importance and weight. Whether her theme is illness, aging, memory, spirituality, sex, love, or the infinite subtleties of one's place and responsibility in the natural world, Galer's poems surprise and affirm with delightful accuracy, humor and empathy our shared experience, our mutual yet unique star stuff.

Equally striking and edifying is Galer's social relevance and playful sense of invention. One meets them everywhere in these poems, especially in the enigmatic *Crooked Path, Crooked Path*, the strange *Under G*, in which the poet riffs on alternate definitions of the words *grebe* and *glebe*, and the powerful *My Seed*, which includes these lines:

> May your rifles twist, your shot curdle. May a web of cloud
>   blur your aim,
> may your arms weigh heavy, your fingers freeze.
>
> And in that moment,
> may you find your conscience delivered before you and
>   bloom,
> my seed.

Another important aspect of Galer's poetry is her fierce commitment to the Divine Feminine. She lives in and speaks for new paradigm Womanhood in ways that do not dismiss the masculine but invite co-creation on more balanced terms than our fading patriarchy has previously allowed. Listen to these lines from *Old Lessons*:

> True fire is a woman.
> Like St. Thomas
> I am ready to recognize the power
> of a female god.

Or these lines from *Night Flying Woman*:

> Deep in the body of a moonless night
> I took my blood and flesh out for a spin.
> I danced in white circles of skin and bone
> and flew, a spray of stars and words
> like a witch come alive
> 'round the dazzling fire.

Jane Galer is an evocative prowler of all that it means to be human in this time and place and in all times, all places. In a real sense, her poems are rituals and incantations inviting us to discover our highest selves, our deepest memories and most exalted intentions for Now, for the future. She invites us to surrender and step into the world as co-players with ravens, dogs, the moon and sun and stars, trees, gardens and ocean tides. Her poems provide inspiring truth that she is trustworthy as a guide, a spiritual friend who sympathetically reads another's heart.

Isn't this the desire of every poet? Isn't this the wish of every reader who comes to poetry with emotional yearning, with a hunger to know what casts light on the path? In recommending this book, which I do with unequivocal joy, I celebrate a true poet, shaman guide and moon priestess with these lines from *Banshee (a spell)*:

> White voice of the Other,
> howler from the heavens,
> bender of trees, caller on the mountain,
> now down my chimney,
> now through the cracks,
> prize open the windows,
> seep beneath the door
> moaning portend, wailing warning.
> Banshee, March mother, wind warrior,
> High Priestess, Death Mistress, Singer of the Bones.
> Firefall, blood bond, white Shewolf,
> Stalker of the quiet world
> bring it down, bring it down.

In her poems, Jane Galer brings it all down to us, the experience of letting go and letting in, of letting be and becoming. What more could we possibly ask poetry to do?

—Robert McDowell

Poet, teacher, speaker and activist Robert McDowell is author of 15 books of poetry, criticism, and the craft of writing. A founder of Story Line Press, he served there as director and editor for more than two decades.

Outskirts

Part 1

Too Deep for Tears

Table of Contents

There are two landscapes of my heart,
both called longing. Chambered valleys.

One, the inner realm, infinitely
black with endless starred sky
where I cartwheel
among questions still unanswered
after all these lives;
a freefall of longing
measured by zodiacal whimsy
my fate to wander.

The chamber opposing:
lush with earthy peat,
unwalkable wet and soft
where I want to lie naked,
my most tender parts
awakened by the furze of new growth,
scarlet and velvet green,
to see clouds above
and know that their shape is Ireland,
her winds swift with poetry and magic tongues.

Elemental

Earth:
The heat, slick and aching for the dark
kindled by your half-shut eyes.
Already I arch and curl,
expand and contract. Essential roundness.
Hurry.

Air:
The mind, my invisible library,
we check out titles, peer over them
together, eager students
rewriting. I know everything
you do not.

Fire:
This lifetime, lessons of survival
and death. Fetch me a midwife
for my soul wanders and still
everyone needs my help.

Water:
The senses, listen
with your whole being.
Until you hear the ocean speak
you won't have used them all.

Harvest Moon

You reign though nothing remains
in the field but straw men and
orange likenesses of your fullest self.
You have exhausted me,
stolen the morning-quiet light,
shadowed the forest with
imaginary bears
and men I could wish for—
highland braves whose skirted knees
 tease and arouse.

You keep me awake all night
with my dreamings, hotter
than Indian summer,
tossing shafts of light
down my favorite oak tree,
grinning at me in your full-face delight.
You have exhausted me,
made me empty and ravenous.

Already I regret the summer's passing,
mourn with the wind that returns
at your command
shaking the trees from their leafy reverie.
You preside as though the veil is a joke
we conjure to cover our lack of experience,
our false dedication.

You shine
and still we cannot read at night.

Leafcurl

My heart unfurls
like tender leaves on a new green stalk—
paper thin,
ruffled at the edges, masking strength
in sinuous unobserved flutterings
held bated,
but nobler by day.

At night my heart's desire enfolds
to a heavy weighted mass
of missing your touch
and thrusts
that have nothing to do with love
and everything to do with binding.

Later, in the deep silence
of our own binary beating pulses,
we are one
filamented
heart.

North Lake Passage

From a rough shore push
a moment's step in icy water,
red rock mooring. What other joy
is as pure: the glide and settle, a cadence of interruption
and flow, mine matching yours.
She Loon watches with a discrete red eye,
dips her beak for a sip
and then straightens her striped glistening neck and cries
Who will love me? as we shiver past.

Night Blooming Jasmine

As if one morning I might
wake to find the house covered,
wrapped tight, jasmine joined
by throbbing tendrils: remnants of the chaotic night,
a disordered gift wrap green and fragrant
and I suspended—yet aging still.

I've been too long watching for growth,
too long waiting for rooted angularity
to bind body to mind.
I've hesitated, paused
within the heavy sweetness of scent.
Now, when the palest flowers parch and drop,
I stand beyond the beveled glass
while night comes with welcome winds.

Wild Wind

I can teach you how dark the wild wind is.
Sling together worlds of gods in likenesses indescribable
desired by the likes of you and me.
While trees buckle and She screams my name,
I can teach you how to slide your darkness into mine
and how fiercely you will want that
from me again and again.
As the moon marshals the blackest clouds aside
and we lie in our gasping
reprieve, we'll look at our slick pricked bodies
and dance the words and laughter
of lust with our fingertips.

The Underside of Leaves

If you turned me
and held me up to the light,
what would you see?
Would you see a tree of perfectly duplicated threads
ever reaching outward, sunwise?
Or would you see collapse: the effect of disturbing
the symmetry of warp to weft?

You would see a haphazard mesh of bone
where tendon and sinew twined like serpents mating
makes a strangulate knotting that threatens to explode
this curse of gene upon gene, aging restlessly
in favor of immediate death.

Drowning Pool

A long languorous dive
into the deep marble-green lagoon
lasts a moment farther into panic than life allows.
Heavy water-laden silk refuses to struggle with me to the surface.
I wonder in that instant
if I should slacken my set jaw,
fill my lungs one last time
with aquatic air.
I play at that for a moment,
bubbles dancing.
The power makes me smile.

Dragging toward the surface, buoyancy fights silkweight,
comet tails of panic in my chest.
Looking up, I see lily pad bottoms dangling their legs,
entangling the hair that seems to be trying to swim away from me.

Darkness arrives in time with the surface,
silk becomes gossamer, easy flight.

While You Were Out

Did you mark the change?
It came, as it inevitably does,
while you were out,
the result of a paragraph,
a stanza, more likely a maudlin
movement of strings
in unison. I am compelled
to follow
folding in on myself
pleated, combed, painted over.
Sometimes I am so mercenary
as to play the pieces again
and again, as if I enjoy melancholy,
resolute in the downward inward turn.
Inside out, I am
when you return.
Raw and unlikable,
I've had the ready smile to tea
and found it wanting in depth,
structural soundness.

While you were out
all my misgivings danced
the fire dance and called for sacrifice:
for the spoken word, at least.
You return and find my face altered
by too many words and too few tears,
and a clawing distance between us
louder than the pipe organ's dominant
resolution.

I can't imagine why you are
invariably startled—you
so used to melodrama uninhibited

by reason, yet here we sit
a word and more between us
passed in a single afternoon
of dangerous inattention.
Now we will begin at the base
and learn again the whys, by touch
and smell and taste.
We will drive all thought into the night
where it belongs, until again,
you are out.

Still Life

An assembly of objects I think will make it full:
a fountain pen of black and shining silver,
a piece of soapstone, an owl from my own hand,
a thick slab of virgin books, the fullness of a peony.
Your love letters than never came.

An impossibility of desires
asking to fix a moment in time
that I can call perfection.

There is an unsettled tension
lying between the flower and the book
in a metaphor of disconnect. Like spider threads
let loose on a summer morning,
as if an illness proposes to rule my world.

If it were easy, a gathering of tendrils
like stalks for a bouquet, it would not be a life.
Yet there is bounty to be had in the trying,
a demented scattering resolved, aligned, at last
into this still and singular journey.

Desire

Lake born waves lick the mossy shore,
rhythmic gentle caresses
like the ones I give you freely,
not the ones we tear from each other
with teeth and shivered skin.

The boat hesitates in wet sand,
a moment's indecision, a shifting
of weight as I mount and settle her.
For balance I'll have the moon;
you can keep your sunshine.

The first dip of oars, a surge of freedom
becomes an easy cadence of glide and drift.
I shed my clothes.
Like ocean birds
they bubble and cling in my wake.

My arms bend to their task,
legs spread, breasts reach and pebble—
beacons for your lighthouse.
Water is my mirror, moonlight is my cloak.
I'm coming for you.

Fishing

My mouth is full of silver, glittering fish.
Several of them biting, sharp and tiny.
I can't help it. They leak
from me, one at a time
slipping slick between wet lips.
They are my beggars.

Were I to batten my lips down tight,
they would crowd my throat,
choked truths,
sleek parcels of love, each
containing a single moment of my heart.

Think of Something Else

Azure, a Persian blue, the sky
our infinite field.
Scarlet, matte or liquid with
lush longing, her lips.
Silver, reflective, blinding
the sharpness of tears.
Emerald, the dense compact, old knowing,
her eyes.
Sable, the silk of chocolate melted,
a plaited river, her hair.
We could do this all day
it would not bring her back.

I'm No Emily

My door opens and air and chaos
chase each other
until disorder insists I have no sharpened pencil,
my ink is dry, parched in fact.
Even in earliest morning
trucks lumber down river grades
stealing my forests, roaring like carnivores,
scaring away coherence.

I'm no Emily
I haven't worn white
since my bridal bower.
Black is my color now,
weeds for days that pass
without a word on paper,
but many spoken, given away
without grace and nary a thought.

I'm no Emily
but like her, I've got piles of notes,
intentions, directions, inflections.
Impatient ghosts line my study walls
queuing for present time,
time I've wasted on games
of chance and superstition, carefully
recorded with religious intensity.

I'm no Emily.
I don't recall the virgin time.
My words scribe the slickness
of blooded pulse,
the way my fingers search for flesh.
I would drop everything,
even my pen,
for another night of mindless frenzy.

Some sense of her solitude
acts as a lure, a stabilizer:
that I can do this at all
closes the door.

Road Kill

Vultures stand sentinel. Restless
row of five, defining
the ditch of the verge.
Ravens three, overhead, mock:
Death here, death here.
Death
here.
The bridge stretches wooden and narrow,
a skid of blood, a red brick of skinned flesh
cast aside,
only the ocean below unperturbed.

Next time, the deer declares
as I watch him rise to the astral,
next time, I'll drive.

The vultures reel and pick
dive and circle,
and scattered by my noisy passage, dive again.
Gleaners
soul takers
midwives
carrion snatchers
their chipped wings barely miss me.
Fearlessly hungry, patient.
Full moon wreckage:
this dreadful ocean highway.

Babies wobble and slide across
the road confused in panic,
down the centerline:
Where is mama?
How long will they live, polka and dot?
So new to this life. Why deer, this time?
Why now, why here?

Each night they die.
Each day the winged giants detail the bones.
Each day I hear them, soaring, calling
roadkillroadkillroadkill.

Riding a Bus Across Jordan

Darkness fueled by dust.
I remember no moonlit sky
no guiding star or threesome.
Just me, alone with all these others
random cut, bizarre child's holiday.
My arms stiff-bracing, body juddering
against the pot-holed bounce and clatter.
The metal bench pinches
like an old man's thumbs.
My thighs sweat and stick.

In the distance, our beacon,
the twinkling rapture of the coca-cola sign.
Even here, when I am at the end of it.
Don't tell me about the promised land,
don't tear up this loneliness and
give it another name,
another face.
Hollow promises:
be that the end.
Lukewarm foaming sweet bottles,
distant music our rapture.
Even sleep is the punishment of heat
riding
a bus across Jordan.

Old Lessons

True fire is a woman.
Like St. Thomas
I am ready to recognize the power
of a female god.
I've learned to quiet the quest for companions,
long to be alone
away from women's chattered sucking in of breath,
energy not freely given.

The fire is not shared. A gift,
it wails up from wombstone
and breastearth, a wailing,
it bursts out the chimney,
not a Banshee within as tradition declares:
Death striding out with fingertips long
and bony. Grasping.

The fire asks the questions,
ignites the challenger. The unknowable
Gnostic Goddess,
demanding her place at the table,
is routed out once again.
With hardened eyes, She asks:
How long yet will we be
alone among women
learning old lessons?

Self-Evidence

Once they were a lush luxurious invitation.
Now they are dowager jugs, canted,
swollen for caress.
Soon they will be hag's cackle—
when the red pill fades,
when the last suckle
tastes a brittle
nipple.

I knew a woman when I was ten

I knew a woman when I was ten
who sat in her garden
through a long afternoon.

She held a glass in her hand
three-quarters full of lemonade.
She was not yet fifty.
The glass was strewn with yellow daisies
frosted with rivulets of chill
working their way to the grass below her hand.

I knew a woman when I was ten,
who sat still in her chair
until the sun painted daisies onto the back of her hand.
I marveled at her stillness.
I laughed at the game the sun played.
She was quiet, barely there.

I knew a woman when I was ten
who learned her breast had betrayed her
and sat still in her garden in August's lush heat
holding her breath,
demanding the sun's touch
as proof she was real.

August Ocean

The struggle to accommodate
spring's moontide river flow
has ended.

The silky sexy smooth ocean
sits languorously
ready at last to be taken.

She curls her finger: venture forth,
come into my turquoise lapis sapphire emerald
froth-lace face.

Green lipped mouth rush
temptation and deception
August ocean, sleeping leviathan.

Marriage

Perhaps we should wonder:
in the solitary glare, so often
our flight an owl's path
unblinking and lone,
what is the glue of our union
now that bridal bowers
and patent vows are reflections
of another skin, another breath?

What keeps the years ours?
What touch that we do not define
sets the pace?
What heart of knowledge ignites
even now, when we join?
What ecstasy of pulse, what
simplest of pleasuring
locks us within
this thing called marriage?

By truth and loyalty it progresses.
By the touch of my mouth,
by the glide of your hand.
By grace and the gods? No,
only by you and me.

I want to know complacency

I want to graft this itch to the faltering druid's oak,
encourage it to flourish, bespell and mystify.
Leave me in peace.
Leave me to reminisce perhaps,
catalog decades of striving,
goals flung aside
an easy tarot deck gawking:
Hanged Man, Empress, Fool.

I want to embrace the wise crone:
persistently ancient is the complacence of her knowledge.
Leave me gray and brittle
to fade and crack
in the fine porcelain of womanhood.
Leave me to shudder with reflections of oncoming pain,
remembered wounds, layered,
layered, a muslin shrouded map of my body's betrayal.

I want to trace a glad heart
as I watch the embers of creativity flutter,
spark and blacken under my breath.
I want to sit back on my haunches by the fire
and know the complacency that comes with the myth of dryness.
My body is a well, not a desert.
I have tears to shed for generations yet.
I have rivers of warmth that glide, bubble and ooze.

I want to know complacency.
One last joyous passion that ends in sweet reverie.
One last hinging of my body to yours,
matching satisfactions.
I want to know the complacence that would come
when your touch is only a gesture from the past,
benign reminder,
no flame kindled.

I want to coast, skate, glide, even fly.
I want to damn them all to hell
and not regret it.
But I suspect that once complacent,
death would surprise me.

Fish Stories

At what point, now
have I learned to parry
with meaningless words?
And is this good
or is the reluctance I feel
going into the room
a signal I should have heeded?

Should I not speak so earnestly?
At length?
Esoterically? (You see how this digresses and sours
as deadly as alcohol in drawing out the bore.)
Should it be so painful?
Fruitless?
Have even I learned anything from these pleasantries
but their unpleasant repercussions
as I lie awake later
and belie the energy lost,
piece together the fragments, strewn bits of soul?
This is shyness itself.
It is at the core of even the smallest efforts,
the simplest of exchanges,
an exchange of energy:
a comparison and trading,
absorbing of power.
The shy one loses.

I'm learning:
keep it simple: this is the essence of charming.
Keep it neutral so as not to brag or preen.
Keep your verbal integrity.
Shyness can be interpreted as aloof
or irritable
or charming
in men always that—charming.
In me?

Shadowplay

Fluttering against the eggshell wall
I can see everything about your image:
the essence of long lithe stem,
curling threads of growth,
waving in the gentle kiss of wind.
Leafshape perfectly formed
again and again along your spine.
I can see your intent: the sun
your struggle: to reach the sill
your nemesis: the wind.
In a moment, clouds steal you away.

My Life Is Like Lake Superior

I am the gentle lapping,
water over pebbles,
soft cascades of shoreline
a repetition of comfort
and easy movement.

But the lake is also deep
and deeply hued.
Changing colors—frosty and blue
rolling and thundering green.
There are steep cliffed heights
with frightening chaos of froth below.
No current of logic
but a continual desperation of waves.

Now and then at evening
the moon can shine across me—
smooth the brow of my green face—
a straight road of pure light,
a bay becalmed by the Mother.

All Hallow's

A share of time,
stars sorted as if for our amusement
alone.
This night time flighting
you, me
and the raven,
awake after dark.

Rejection

It's not core,
as if you said my breasts were too small
or that we did not fit, my fault
or yours.
A life has not been taken
or taken up.
All that it is
is a scattering of words
on a snowstorm drift of pages
tossed, rejected—
like the cascade of my spine,
vertebrae crumbling too soon,
in anticipation of endings.
A deck of cards, these words,
a tarot of the faults we call our tribe.
Words between us scorned
after being so proudly loved.

Burial at Navarro

I came back later,
stilled by the vastness,
this her watery grave,
saddened once more by the loss of her earthbound presence.

The seals who had met our entrance
with appointed attention—six sleek gleeful pallbearers—
were lounging out to sea
on rocks, untouchable.

The river flows with determined speed
no matter the tidefall,
past sentinel rocks,
gulls hovering.

Where was she, I wondered?
Where will she be.

The fine gray dust of death sprayed over us.
I tasted her bones, I covered my face in her ash.
I was frightened that her escape into the sea
would steal the last of her from me.

Out with current she spread with her escorts
cheerfully diving, twirling, turning
out to meet the waiting whales, accompany their birth quest,
south to warm waters.

Constancy

What are violets
but a flower I cannot keep in bloom?
An energy of loyalty
that ages to velvet gray,
petals long gone, without the grace
to fade.

I remember the vivid purple of royalty—
a sun, you were its center.
I nestled against your shine,
my darkness richly colored,
overlapped, petalled
and caressed—you stood
upright for me
magnanimous in your loving.

Now some of me is pale and brittle.
My enfolding
is a careful dance to old steps,
flameful memories.
Some of me is barely there,
velvet rubbed off,
worn too much, just too much.
Without the purpose to go
I remain
constant to your center.
Longing for the scentless flower,
we should go to sleep at night
like poppies.

Death in the Afternoon

I teetered briefly in a moment of this afternoon
in the void at the edge of reason
where all life is questioned.
Because reasoning works against us
when we can see so many sides to life as we've lived it,
suddenly it is null.

Can the clue to survival
be to live for the moment and that moment's future?
Because we cannot justify the now
by the then,
childhood by our parents
adulthood by our friends?

Our conclusion must be chaos:
unrelated, unreasoned events
strung together with genetic glue
in so haphazard a way
that meaning cannot endure
from one decade to the next.

Looking for an Omen

Spotted or pygmy,
unwisely, an owl.
Perched, curious or stunned
on the kitchen oak, too low.
All gray matter and feather plume,
yellow eyes and stillness.
Is it chance or design
that brings you down to my level?

Where's the one booming all night?
The one calling
all those questions,
perfect echoes?
Where's the flap and thump
of air, wingspan terrifying?
Why are you here,
small surrogate or accidental tourist?

I'm looking for an omen, not a nudge,
cataclysm or thunder strike
is what I need now.
You're just confusing me,
vulnerable and rare.
We are kin, masters of
small truths or platitudes. We are
earthbound hunters, ground huggers
philosophers unblinking.

Motherhood

I sound more and more like my mother
talking to this child-grown man,
in a voice of mothers-all.
Not my own, not me,

cajoling with every line,
yet keeping something back for my pride
unsuccessfully,
giving away my heart
again in every breath.

Trapped between generations
of expectations
I am frozen without power,
pinballed between one who knows all and is forgetting
and the one who knows little
but remembers it all.

As this time presses me into the mold that is myself
I lose the ability to defend myself—
the capacity to extend myself.
I look around me for physical shelter,
but the onslaught of the generations
demands more of me than is safe to give.

Chunks of certainly fall away.
I kick them aside
before I am nothing,
breathing inward,
hoping for someone to remain constant,
fearful of new growth.

Adagio in G Minor Father and Me

We seem to have said our peace,
premature to soul's improvement,
spurred on by adjacent deaths
measured in slices of our hearts.
We monopolized each other's minds—
daily catalogs of rememberings—
as we divided up the things
we once craved,
the house vibrating to strings and organ
overwhelming.
(I could not have spoken anyway
through choked breath and tears.)
Our own adagio danced
around champagne glasses and old silver,
our possession of memories has blurred
as if your wedding photo is now mine:
the slip of satin candlelight,
the gentle wise smile, smoke black hair,
our regrets.
All these entwined hazards
we've put to rest
too painful to open daily now
that life has miraculously continued.
And so we drifted into polite acceptance
like an old coat, a friend, slipped
around your shoulders,
no need for speech.

Reunion

This first shot is the lake:
frothed over with a northerly blow.
Most of you don't recall
the loose board on the dock
the submerged tree our monster,
chipmunks and daddy longlegs,
the smell of army canvas,
or wet and sandy bottoms.

Somehow we are here to teach
you these memories.
Make you taste and smell
our childhoods;
marry them to your own
nascent ones. Beg you
to fold and refold our sense of clan,
an internal face.
Carry it along,
just as you do that blunt end nose,
perfect pitch, left hand blue eyed
toe curling, freckled
tangle of us all.

Shelter

A forest of hasty trees,
narrowly rooted, part slightly and
beckon with a deer path through
second growth.
No matter.
Once there, in my forest grove,
the smallest wasting log lies
spiked and painted with vivid mosses,
primeval throne.

Tipping back my head,
ravens mark me, criticize,
passing.
I can sink deep here,
open wounds,
anchor errant fear in some other
simpler shape.
The trees weep for me in swift swirling fog.

The jersey cat comes to lead me home.

Eclipse

I watched your hovering dimness
and feared you would not recover.
In my heart, I knew the world was flat,
love was scarce,
longing tenacious.

And so I searched the moon-dark sky for reassurance
but wasn't convinced you would care to return,
any more than I am sure of loyalty,
faith,
the power of truth.

I will not speak these questions.
My mouth closes,
pursed grimly
determined to wait,
motionless.

Rather than honor your house in shadow
(I cannot meditate on your rebirth)
I wait in suspended thought
breath held in uneasy pattern,
thoughts in disarray.

What relief when I sense the time is ending.
A cricket responds to the reflection of its own body in the water
and confused, thinks to mate.
Rustling below in the gentle swale
tells me a bird resumes her nest-building.

The revealing glow reassures me by measures:
I will own again my bold fecund harvest moon.
I will feel again its power, its seduction.
Triumphant I will bare my aging breasts
and marvel at their beauty in moon's perfect light.

February

I.
I don't like February.
Not because the ice in the gutter is thick and gray and deeply
   suspicious.
Not because the lingering snow yields for a moment, tempting me,
as if paid by vegetable seed packers to make me think spring is near
   to hand.
Not because its dearth of days belies the dreadful reality
that the season of celebrations is over:
the last Christmas gift arrived weeks ago,
the last of the New Year's cheer drunk one recent night,
cast aside with our inhibitions—
poor Robbie Burns, his loves and lusts unchecked.
Ah, yes, and the hearts and flowers came and went with a pathetic
   rapidity,
hallmark of a dying tradition.
Oh, you say, did you want something?
Oh, I sigh to myself, how shall we kindle the fire this time?

And then to top it off,
this February has lost its full moon, robbed of it,
ashamed to show its face in a month so rare in future,
so mean in delight.

II.
I don't like February,
my month of mourning.
The feeling creeps up on me.
There's January dribbling on interminably.
We lockstep into a rote sustaining haze
that just might get us through the winter without incident
and then,
this feeling of edge becomes a disconcerting bag of seers scents
growing deep in my chest, pushing on my heart.

This feeling sometime around the full moon of January last,
takes conscious flight and bashes me in the back
with wings of soft span,
encircles me in a coat of sadness.
Not dark,
but bright jewel hews of purest ruby amethyst and emerald,
my aura becomes thick with sparkling moaning lament.

III.
This is the month of my mother's birth.
It is her birth time, not her death time that brings her
so vividly back into my presence.
This is good.
But it is also all encompassing,
distracting: body and mind shifting.
I take on her life for this short month
as if in some agreement I said that I would.
I think about how she would see,
what she would say.
I hear her voice answer the telephone.
Hello.
Not in anticipation, but rather a deep throaty resignation
that she must connect, and possibly hear bad news.
Again.

I miss her. I miss her. I miss her.
I hear her argue her causes and I wonder that so little has changed.
I look at my body and watch my breasts become her breasts,
my skin become her skin.
I am doomed to wear her mortal imprint.

And then February passes, and the sculptured shell of her
falls away with the brightness
as spring comes again.

Black Swan/Eala Dubh

I am the Measurer: there is a catalog of these things
we've said before, and I am its keeper.
I am the Siren: to me your lust will always prevail,
we are scented one to the other.
I am Queen where no mere goddess will answer,
for we must all be first in our own hearts.
I am the Wanderer because He does not exist
and we have had to invent him or die.
I am the Spinner: for men's minds still reel
at the power of the flowing circle, the pricked finger,
three drops of red on my own breast.
I am the one who shatters and scatters thought and logic.
I can pull the wind behind me more fiercely
than the last time you came to me for advice.
I am the Moon: the earth's true ruler, I can call an army
of all women to my side with a single tide, yet
I am the muted Swan, alone,
chasing an ethereal partner.

Peace Arbor

Let loose the feminine Spirit.
Her vessel the sky,
her roots her own body:
carrier of us all.
Like a girl, all innocent desire
it seems a simple thing:
this peace she seeks.

Reach and arc.
Stem the ache inside;
build outward from your inner light.
Make your vessel the sky—
three worlds enjoined,
bearing.

Heart Dance

Meet me
cloaked as Raven
and I'll teach you to dance.
Meet me
on a mountain top
never mind your broken heart.

Air Dragon

This cascade is Serpent.
Let her fill you, embrace you,
shed the broken shards of old dreams.
Her path is of the Mother
reflective of earth's contour
no straight plane
not even within your own heart.
Her path is the night bird's soaring
a knowing chaos of stars and fire.
She sees nothing
everything
her instinct a dry fire crackling.
She is serpent and womanform
healer and shapeshifter
doubled and torn.
She is flight itself,
the air of breathing and death
angel worn and desperate,
a mountain called and answering.

Guarding the Shamans

South:
A Serpent.
What appears is devastation.
We can shed this fate,
join me in the waters.

West:
A Jaguar.
What you think may get you killed.
Walk across the bridge of bones,
take the lesser path.

North:
A Hummingbird.
When intuition speaks, you must listen.
I drink deeply of the nectar,
but I understand the journey is long.
Be quick.

East:
An Eagle.
We are one, you are foolish to think otherwise.
Under my wing, everything
everything is possible.

Spirit Song

The song of my heart
is the furious joy of mother earth,
the pulsing, measure by measure
of latent dreaming.
My becoming is a fan of shifting bodies tumbling,
a skyward exhale of all of us
as One.
The song of my spirit
tells you my lineage, generations
of grandmothers birthed in patterns
called forth by universal decree:
We are of the People of the Moon.
Flight is our breathing
the sky is our womb.

Burning Seed

You want me this way:
nakedness my feathered cloak.
I am happy to oblige
yet you see, as you must,
where it lies for us?
Painted cycles, a regular moon
of forgiveness and burn.

Yet you want me posed:
splayed and fecund,
a perfection akin to your dreaming.
You want me this way
all newness and posturing
the touch
forgotten.

Flowering Figure

When you watch me like that
I open, reflecting
the heat of your gaze
petalling, so glad for the sun
his caress a breath
across dark nipples.
No need for touch
just your watching is enough
for my flowering.

Hold Your Heart High

I came a thunderbolt:
the sky filled and quavered.
Light threaded like serpents
mating in a storm,
an anguish of pleasure.

How you are able to touch me this way,
deeper than the roots of furrowed field
no order to this passion.
I care not.
I will try to return your gaze.

You have taken me
filled my body.
A flight path of soaring blood:
my heart yours
a sunrise of spent passion
giving birth to my beginning.

The Nap

Sometimes I can call to you
dreaming or not,
and your arrival is a cry and a shudder
as even in sleep my hands
caress and soothe.

Your whispers
are the language of the wisest moments.
I wish I could recall your speaking,
but waking, you've left me
satisfied again, without
needing further wisdom—
your warmth and dark softness
enough.

Midlife

There was a time I might have gladly asked
your opinion—
might have considered that half
of all this is yours, rightfully,
but it began to divide
my physical self—requiring too much energy—
that posturing of woman and wife.

When nights came and ripeness
was a reminder of my fullest self,
a reminder of who I was before I lay out
for you, before the moon was full
and union became compromise,
then I knew to recognize
the taste of life.

Open Heart

I lap over you
like the seasons:
the dread of fall, ghost
of winter, the sweet
berryness of summer
flooding of spring.

There is a chaos
to our chambers,
oblivious as we are
to the sound of thunder,
to crash of wave.

We lay it open
and swim on.

Wild Horses and Ravens

I can if I wish
take your heart from your breast.
As the serpent glides and schemes
I can tongue deep in you,
and with my hand, hold you—
your power resolved into
a single stiffness,
your cry a raven's call
of pleasure.

Hands in Flight

If the Mother cradled you again
she would show you
in the lined map of her palms
the length of this journey
not perhaps half done.

But what would be changed
with a knowing outcome?
A distance made less
by being already a notion or intent.
With fire in your head
your path follows the ancestors:
the She-guide lures and beckons.

Until you are filled,
filled—
you are not finished.

Binding

If, as you say,
we were to prove the luminous thread
that holds a ripened seed
in thrall to a waxing moon,
would our power double
or treble?
Would the earth promise
to warm me,
shelter and protect?
Or would there always be naysayers,
skeptics and fools
men who would clothe me.

Spirit Vessel

In my dreaming
I am constantly searching for you.
What is it that fills my grail
with a perfume so strong,
so tantalizing
that I waken glistening:
the combined essential oils of
love and destiny and spirit
still scenting my awakening.
Yet, so far, the grail
is only a wanderer's deep valley:
moments of inspiration that flutter
and glide.
Still, the whole perfection contained
within.

Swimming with the Moon

Strange brew
Her cosmic creation.
Amniotic mire:
we come full fashioned,
at swim beneath her sea.
Shell cast
we threaten perfection
yet we cannot touch.

Too soon
too soon to reveal
Her plan.

Tree of Life

When Raven called us to him
he cried a moon raving
for us to follow.
And we saw
that his heart was a girl
newly formed.
An opportunity, he said,
for us to return. At any moment
before death
we can recall, reseed.
We can follow his flight
and become the girl
newly taken,
aware of only her own
spell.

Flight with Raven

It's a philosophy, isn't it?
Yet somehow, Grandmother,
you have had a hand in the flying.
I think you cast your spell
long ago:
When the sea had eyes,
when the wind spoke to you
in spirals,
when Raven could tell tales
of your yearnings.

You told us to be strong,
follow the cycle.
You gave us your own knowing
and the Moon herself
was brighter for our power.

Earthcasting

Beloved:
You must see our mirrored reflections
even, or perhaps particularly,
in Death.
The similarities are striking.
Our tribes overlapping millennial
structures, woven with brittle thread.

Yet, struggle as we do,
it does not seem to break,
this passionate bond—
you to me
us to Earth.
Her creatures, we have no wings
yet nightly, now, we can fly.

Three Ravens

Three because the world has three centers:
As long as they are still in flight
we will not have found our way.

Bog Slip

A crayon sky blue dingy,
green water three inches deep in the bottom—
mirror of stillness.
Focus of all longing.

Tethered to the reedy bog
she waits,
undulating to the gentle wave-tune
oarless. I am stranded.

Glare like shining muslin webs
hides the distant magic isle.
My eyes squint and strain
for detail. For a future notion.

Does that opalescent mound,
scant of tree, tumble of rock and heather,
harbor opportunity?
I should always think so.

Ireland

We should stride toward the beckoning ocean.
We should stand at the cliff edge, straining,
so close our breath is a falling.
We should face east
and push,

push with our hearts
till the continent moves
or
moves within us the distance of safety, and
straps us furrowed against rumors of wind sweep.

We should sway into the lure of wave-crash
and holler for braver souls
who swim below the green-froth—
who ride selkie's slick whorish length
and abandon us to this fate.

We are brittle cowards,
thistle, shamrock
crushed, weary
wintered over.
There is no end.

Solar Earth

Storm,
what happens when the earth
confuses her seasons?
While roses wash with chill
iris billow and break.
When rain comes sideways
rooted trees, ancient,
relax. Quaver.

What happens when March
winds never come?
Sea birds hunker
longing for vibrant air.
A gray ocean rises
awash with castings:
logs thrown off
a churned riverbed in anger.

The earth, a folding.

Tack

Night sky black with shining sweat,
a ripple of shivering chill
across the long muscled flank.
Leather strapping scrapes. Brass buckles
collide, separate
and collide again.
The earth is measured by roundness—
the soughing sound of the horse's great exhale,
the creak of harness paired and settled.
Blind impatience, shifting heat.

Passage Tomb Dance

This barren moonscape
birthed jagged rocks—
shards struck at angles.
They tumble here from God's hand—
splintered dice
thrown in a losing pitch.

A plateau slab:
Diarmuid's bed.
Grainne's sleek form dances
a crystaled nightsky step.
She lifts her arms
heavenward,
keening.

The Mermaid's House

You are wrong to think of it under water.
It rides the cliff-face.
She perches at its scaled rooftop
surveying her domain, her right hand
the keen eye of an osprey.
She watches every lash of wave,
every moment of foaming crest,
she wiggles, delighted, at whalespout.
She frowns at motor roar, despising
the pounding of reverberation beneath her fin.

She looks always for lovers.
Her mission is to lure,
to impale their souls on jagged rocks,
lift their wanting bodies to her shelter.
She offers them full breasts of hungers
satisfying.
She knows their willingness:
for a sea moment with her
they will turn their backs on everything:
ship, shelter, womankind.

She keeps their memories
like libraries of leathery relics;
and sometimes she floats by
the chamber of their secrets
and turns the page
just to hear them cry out.
She will tie them up in ringlet hair
and make them hard and mindless.
With soft laughter bubbles
she will close tightly over them,
stealing the air of their pleasured smiles.

When she tires of them,
she throws them off the cliff and watches
her ocean toss their naked bodies,
a rhythm of pale limp warnings
men never heed.

Exiles

And so they say of us
are we voyagers or seekers,
misfits or isolates? We suffer
ninth wave disaffection, as
countryless wanderers we are
old lives haunting airy chambers:
silver rings, echoes of fabled losses,
tokens of a dialogue for seers—
between us a cachement
of truths refolded
to our liking.

The Lure

On the riverbend rock
she twists her torso and
shows him her sweet glistening breasts.

I'll just be coming there ... says the lad.
And he jumps from the heathered bogside
into the water.

The mermaid chuckles,
and peers over the rocks as he surfaces
beneath her gaze.
Her laughter cascades around his ears.
He sputters for breath, scrambles for a hand up.

Her twinkling laughter disappears into a sigh
as she rolls onto her back and off the rock.
Diving deep
below him she goes as she whispers
Let me help you

The Winter Queen

I.
Childish penchants for horseback
led her mornings to the market
of horse stalls sleek and gleaming.
Loose and pent-up
underneath her wools and linens,
she knew them.
She chuckled to each one
and picked her mount by their
answering
stamp of anticipation.

Soon enough it seemed to her
her body betrayed her
with small biscuit breasts
hard and hot
like flints against the linen,
a goading, stabbing of maidenhood.
Blood showed with the moon
a burning thread within cutting,
rending childhood.

Childish ways were set aside.
The smell of womanskin
led men to her side,
and caused women to stare,
chattering behind bijoux fingers,
counting her chances like petals.

Her will deserted her.
Her hair went straight.
Roped in pearls wrapped round tight,
all girlhood silken ribbons of paler hues
gone, left behind, dead snakes strewn
across stone floors cold.

She thought she would never be warm again.
And though she did not yet see why,
she sat before the fire frowning,
piecing together the fabric of her future
as Queen.

II.

In shadows men posed—
emissaries, advisories, missionaries,
warring
poets, admirers, lover's apprentice
fawning—
no womanfolk, midwife, healer or confessor for
consoling.

She is the forward looking queen.
This boned brilliant horizon
a catapult, her body within.
She fingers long strands
and sometimes they break:
pearls scatter at her army's feet.
They, on their knees,
chase pearls in chaos
and raise their eyes expectantly
as one anonymous hungry man.

She has her favorite.
He knows power of place,
the one who would not fawn.
(If they had only known it was this easy,
the others cried, smacking their heads.)

When presented at court
with a flourishing bow,
he swept the plumed cap

across the stone floor
and brushed the white skin
of her foot, its feather a tickle.
It shot an arrow, touched the secret burning thread.
She started—eyes wide—met his almost smile
and knew him.

III.
Sometimes she stands barefoot
at the edge of heat,
toes splayed, gripping beasts—
the only parts of her unadorned.
She hopes an errant spark will fly,
eat its way outward
next to the silksewn pearls
and satined silver,
a black worm of temptation,
it might fall just at the crease,
white and delicate
where her toes join and
she could smother it,
a black smear of coal,
her other foot to feel,
ah, to feel something
like heat.

After prolonged moments
with eminent emissaries
she huffs out her brocade sails
and kicks off thimble slippers,
curling her toes like babes,
and acquiesces to the very next request,
startling even her ministers
with the craftiness of her caprice.

Once or twice she can't resist
and goes unbound and slipping
down spiral stones, shoeless,
grateful, for once in her life,
for the wholeness of the man
waiting, waiting behind the bold oak door.
And when he doesn't bow, but lifts
the hem of her gown and reaches
for her with warm extended fingers,
her toes blaze
and she cannot return
the clarity she sees in his eyes.

IV.
Advisors surround her, a windy
black forest of men.
Her frown deepens,
fingers narrow and wrinkle,
they have so little to do.
Doubt is her sworn enemy.
Her blood reward withers
passion long ago denied,
a distant memory of flare.
Spite comes in its place.

She banished her poet,
murdered her lover,
quarreled her agents from the hall.
The ache inside has become her tyrant,
a scourge. At last, she is wholly her own:
the lute player's daughter,
her palms marked with teeth.

The Piper

His face lies in my thoughts,
an uneasy song.
His plaintive rising sound
stays near as I leave.
Ireland's piper
holds my mind.
They say Ireland's a woman
—wild haired, reddened cheeked.
Ireland's a man.
—Coarse wide hand
caressing my pale breast,
speaking softly of tears shed,
loves past.
Playing his pipes,
not meeting my gaze
laughing.

Shaughran/Wanderer

It's not the scholar or ascetic's quest
I follow. I am not hollow
footsteps in ancient halls
clouded with musty words,
or endless barefoot paths
of thorny devotion
searching out a forgiving god
where there is none.

I seek the perfect moment
in place and time: the instant
of absolute blooming
where my nose touches the butter-yellow blossom
and is gifted with the finest sense of rose.
I'm gathering opportunity,
chances for the perfect wave set,
the one that causes all these birds
to huddle fearfully on the sand.
I am counting on the sight of a finger of lake
a castle ruin at its head just
at the earliest moment of morning tide
where all life is still
enshrouded in sea mist.

I'm collecting these perfections
against the crumbling threat, the time
when I will sit still, at last,
and spread my collection before me
in the sweet wandering that is memory.

Grandmother

Maggie, thirteen and pert in Sunday checks,
sits upright in a potato patch.
Her face says "I'm going from here."
Her father stands over her right shoulder,
one thumb stuck jauntily in his trouser band,
the other playfully balances a pitchfork near the potato mound.
His face says "I am from here."
His new wife leans toward his side.

He wasn't a farmer, was this a lark?
A postcard of traditional leave-taking?
Gram's ship waiting dockside
while they pose with potatoes,
as if a moment in history
can speak for a whole people,
can speak for the Irish.

Alaïs

I followed her down the forest path.
Alice, Alaïs, Alish girl.
Behind me trees held hands
to block my escape.

(Alice strayed down a rabbit hole,
Well, you know ...)

Mixed up? Bemused?
Grow up! Trees yelled.

When all these Alice girls
retreat to their bower,
will you?
For life calls you to this hour.
Put down the image you tore from
a tarot card.
Look full into the mirror and ask it nothing.

(Here and now, Alice,
here and now. Run.
Don't run.)

The Ladies of Blasket Island

Straight gray stones gather watching on the hillside.
Walls curving in wide skirts,
crinolined windows waiting for the sea to give up their men.

Fallen now to ruin,
they maintain vigil,
whispering lies to windblown sheep
who bah carefully to their young in soft panic.

Take this island not for granted.
She works her magic in fierce waves.
Stand forever, widowed huts.
Tell us not to let time pass too quickly.

Gray mists fold softly
until harsh winds consume all life.
Stone houses pinch their faces to the binding of the wind.
And breath holds.

The Basketmaker

Creels stand ready
for shawl-wrapped seaweed gatherers.
With heavy loads they struggle against the seamless rain.

Willow rods pulled from the sally garden
spike in bunches at the ready
like ladies along the dancehall wall.

Weaver of rods—
tap, push, snap, tap—
building a burden
for an ancient tradition.
Weaver of rods—
tap, push, snap—
Winding the unbending
willing shape.
Twining this day to the last.

Bog Cotton

Snow white puffs of whispers
tendered briefly across the summer bog
tell ancient tales to their mistress wind.

Hush.
Listen to their hearts break.

Road to Gravestones

Stark black widows stand straight and still
over a low stone wall circling the churchyard.
Battered arms reach blindly in melting rains.
They seem to move softly in unison in shades of gray
then sparkling granite.
They murmur amongst themselves
in words only faeries can hear.
Shifting slightly as the cloud passing overhead
straightens their hooded brows and lifts their peaks,
we pass by and their shapes define,
their murmurs cease.

Vigilant crosses, spirits stilled,
secrets safe.

The Sally Garden

Will you take me there, my love?
Off the lane, reeds dancing.
Waves splash at the lake's edge.
Will you take me there?
Will you tend me as you tend your garden?
Reeds for baskets twined,
mastered by your hands,
I will be.

Preservation Chapel

Look, she watches you:
the long tenacious-fingered heiress of your faith.
Is she smirking?
Is she serene?
Have you stared deeply into her ruby glass eyes?
Let your vision blur?
Absorb the glittered light?

Or are you contemplating dinner and a pint?

Either is blessed work
if you wish.

The Fisher Man's Lover

She is there every morning he is not,
materializing with the misty dawn,
leaning carelessly against the sea wall.
Gulls overhead
describe their dinner order
until they see she has no means
and other intentions.

She knits while she waits.
In her head a pattern combines today's heartbeat
with the yesterdays of her ancient sisters.
They also stood at this wall,
knitting charms into sweaters for dangerous work.

Celtic cross, ridge and furrow,
berries, ropes, rigging, ladders.
Then, more seriously,
marriage lines, tree of life.
She counts the stitches,
the pattern appears,
but she never looks at her work.
Her fingers glide, she is a graceful conductor.

She looks to the sea
as if any moment her lover will appear,
a small chalice the ocean bears
carrying her fisher man to shore.
The mermaid cautions:
Drink, for soon he'll be away again.
(The mermaid's hand draws too near his face.)

The girl pauses at her task.
Her eyes mingle tears salt and wind.
Her heart fills with the importance of being loved.
Her hands return to their work
as if this is necessary,
as if these threads are the keepers of her lover's fate.

The Seasons of Women

Áine, my brightness,
will you take measure of the sun today?
At last we are shadowless at noon.
Fixed, pausing
while the ancient apple trees fill and reach,
gnarled boughs too old for goldens.

Áine, my faerie
of the horsetail and nettle grove, you are
swift and moon struck.
The little plaster ballerina makes you laugh
even with the lion's marks.
What strange wings
that cannot twitch or fly, you say:
we are beginners.

Áine, my queen,
did you watch the lion in your grove
bite the gnome and find him stone?
Did you laugh your peeling, sparkling ring
and did he turn and run?

Áine, my mistress
your funeral procession passes by. Dancers
spiral silvery fruited wands.
Of grace and beauty
you were renowned.
Come dawn, shall we leave you to this sacred place?

Áine, my goddess,
we turn our faces to the starry sky,
St John's wort pillowed on our tattooed breasts
and smiling, hear your whispered story
as deep silence fills the forest night.
Only your familiar, Owl, remains alert.
In sleep
we'll fly with you.

Absent from Your Gaze

I'm always trying to explain
missing you.
I want
to see you just now, at this moment,
here in this place,
not ours
where gestures molder and warp,
where we ignore the smaller breaths
and sighs. Where the beginning
and end of things is unclear.

I want you here
in this flowing of wheat field,
old stone and cross,
where you might be kindled to my flame again,
moth to my brightness.

I want you in ways I cannot say
without sounding dissatisfied,
for I am not
only searching for moments
of extraordinary pulse
with you.
Yet here I am
missing you
absent from your gaze.

The Old Place

Here is where longing begins.
Here is the core of my remembering.
The first day of spring is not a date.
It is this wind's soft touch,
this sally mist,
this lacey veil—
a muslin shroud of sheerest weight,
like a careful screen over the aging earth.

This coast, this ocean;
connect seeing it today
with the first sight of it,
and it is my own once again.

Breakfast

Ah. There you are now.
Pulled knee high boots
over peat brown corduroy—
trousers shiny, worn in delicate spaces,
quiet places. Not yet clean,
but your body is
smelling fresh and smoky, all of a piece
from where those trousers lay
before the hearthfire last night.

Tell me what you'd say
were you to whisper in my ear
of things your heart speaks
low, yet clear.
Would you quote Yeats?
Say hopes, pray dreams, lob jests,
sing love
to me, all?

With two fingers you push my hair aside,
my neck glows under your breath,
your hand falling away from my waist,
my hip covered, a moment.
I turn to see you leave
through the half-light of the doorway
closing,
your words slung within you,
a noiseless exhale.

Across the lane, not hurried,
not lazy, your practiced whistle leads
the fat generously milked cows through the first gate.
On your face I still see the tumble and trouble
of last night's lovemaking,
a thousand years of poetry,
and a longing for whiskey
to stave off the morning chill.

Beltaney Stone Circle

How through this slot
my soul may skitter
bravely away from warmth and shelter?

Small space
horizon high.
How does it twirl
how does it fly?

This is a twined starry sky;
a cat's paw moon, it suits me well
stillness snugly cloaks us all.

Ha! Where and how will you leave this flesh?
A shooting star?
A gasping breath?

Kilmainham Gaol

Echo of iron, shiver of stone,
did they fear their sacrifice would go unnoticed?
They should not have wondered.
The flower of Ireland feeds on this
misery palpable.
A delicate triptych of cowardly yellow
peaks out from the crack in the wall above
where their bodies exploded.
Did they look up?
Was it their last sight before the hood?
Before the sick one was strapped to the chair,
before his soul was blown heavenward?
Pathetic flower. For freedom
for never forgetting. Oppressed
by Kilmainham's stones, we long for
the flower.

Stone Cottage

Stones profited against wind's will
offer shelter to the weary heart.

Eire gathers her grassy cloak
to her pale form and cries:

Stop here, dear friend,
for solace lies deep with
this ancient mother ground.

Moonbeams

They are there at my Georgian window,
huge and white,
tearing the grasses,
rustling the hedges.

Great pale cows
flicking tails gently over placid rumps,
bellies full of waiting calf.
Descending milk,
building weight.

They look only briefly toward my window,
with quiet acceptance,
breathe evenly, heavily,
and move on.

Belfast News

Jane Peoples, age 116 years.
She retained her sight
and senses to the last. (Belfast News 1880)

We'd like, all of us
to be Jane:
looking at death clear headed
even as bones and sinew shatter
stretch and bake.

We'd like to age
in the manner of an antique vase
the paling of porcelain
only serving to make our worth
noteworthy, increase our value.

We'd like to put the serpent of fear
to rest with long past trials,
face our becoming bold
and bare.

We'd like to hide—
avoid the hospital doors
automatic with regrets,
and die in our sleeping selves
where the light always did shine.

And when one of us does fly
the high-wire act of faith
we shrug and blink and
looking at the odds
count our chances rare,

As even the irreligious
cross themselves in despair.

Children's Spell—Trochos

Egg & apple, moon & breast
Perfect spiral, circles best.
Spinners waulkers fullers friends
Gather now we'll make amends.

Circle dancing take my hand
Pass me deosil 'round the land.
Lifting voices, breasts unfurled
Dancing, dancing ribbons curl.

Acorn, hawthorn, wort and berry
Forgive, forget, forfend. Make merry!

Part 2

The Spirit Birds

Everything Has Changed

Everything has changed. The slow clock descending.
Inside, my heart taps like impatient fingers, disengaged
from this thing called time.
What do you do when there is no spring thaw?
This is that unfortunate month, a daily melancholy.
Everything has changed. We are closer, skin to skin
our bond sealed in a wet wax of bossed golden,
a delicate line flighted through so many years, now strong cord.
Everything has changed. From here, tentative steps retrace
the arcs of living this lifetime without the fear
that comes with disease. We start again but uncertainty rules.
Everything has changed. My notion of what will come
expired like a fairy cloud blown sideways in the wind.
The pale shrouded Boredom hovers over the hag called Fear.
I should thank her for that, instead
I find I cannot just be, this moment is too large for me.
Everything has changed. Between each of us hang the words,
some things should never be written down.

Mostly, I'd rather go to Croatia

Sometimes we delay the act of choice until delaying is the act
and redemption is something we have exchanged for inertia.
Like the time I floated above the acupuncture table,
a conjurer's assistant, and he said,
well, we'd best not do that again.
As if there are edges to this dimension we dare not master.
But I'd like to fly there, Croatia, or those other river capitals,
would it be the stepping back we imagine?
A Transylvania cart-road, this true life type,
like a font scribed out of line of sight,
invisible, like the lines that tether us back and forward,
back and forward between past and destiny.

Mostly, I'd rather go to Croatia
drink beer and eat fatted sausages and wonder
at the sounds of what language? Forget my own.
Rather go than experiment with the surgeon's knife,
literal conjurer, expunger;
he doesn't even have the levitation down.
I could teach him a thing or two,
but I will be invisible then, and no one ever heeds invisibility.
Stripped of golden and gloss, unwrapped and pale, thinking up
five or six lines with which to describe my entire self,
and no, I cannot name all the capitals of the Danube,
I'm leaving that to you.

Constellation

Today the ocean fog is a still and pale valence,
a settling, descending across the conscious mind
until the spaces outside these windows are opaque
with the mirrored fright of not caring.

We count the days between eclipse and caution
all the while knowing no caution is enough.
This is Fate, this while we spend suspended,
a capacious space of nothing we allow ourselves—

a falling. There is a Constellation
with my name on it. All these steps
are a part of that trajectory. No options of worth
matter from year to year.

This fog comes and goes,
a wavelength, a sentence, a minute bit of promise;
a milky disinterested calm
that has descended by my will.

Somewhere else the bright sun disappeared
and all day I've been wondering what awe
feels like. Where is the root of power and majesty?
Where is the line between me and my star?

What is the One thing that will bring us to our knees?

Wandering Around This Thing Called Worry

It is a counter-clockwise motion:
you step outside of time for this worrying path
and circling the small intense house of it,
—barefoot and head down—
you don't see the spectacular star
or hear the tail of awakened song.
Just when you needed it most
nothing soft, supple and generous
finds its way into your arms.

It is a counter-clockwise motion
and all you can ask objectively
is what did they call it before there were clocks?
Disequilibrium, disenchantment
enjambment of the heart,
this thing called worry. Fates
called up as ushers and groomsmen
as the Bride of Death weaves her arbitrary threads
and we spider through a maze of our own making.

Wandering around this thing called worry
wishing for the warning cry
the hawk in her scrying,
moonwise, backwards, dying.
What matters more at this moment? The path,
the smothered promise, or some indecent tally,
a record of our worryings, the threads like November leaves,
an exhaustion of some secret record keeper,
a labyrinth game with dice of bone.

Deconstructing Words

I want you to know the edges of the word desperate.
They are smooth the way fear slithers down your spine.
They are scalpel sharp and at one edge they dare you to test
your sense of courage,
at the other they invite you to creep away, hide beneath
the fallen leaves, crisp winter cover.
Take a match to the word desperate, find the smaller bit, despair,
decompress—an implosion of the heart, a trail of smoke
the whisper of an extinguished flame.
The edges of the words we cannot speak, the choking
balmless blindness of us,
what geometry saves your life?

Waiting

Even at midday, the sun only manages to exaggerate
as long shadows of water willow and pine
tattoo across winter grass.
We are suspicious of a blue cloudless sky,
that will be the time to come.
Waiting to heal a tumorless cavity, an earth breast burned
and burning,
no comfort now, all questioning. Nothing
about this scene will change,
the woodpecker still tending his sap lines,
no lessons learned.

Like the ocean, waves of varying meter plunge and topple,
relentless, like memory, we are called to account.
There will be a moment when all chance ends,
there will be only a small half breath of recognition.
The shadows will lessen making the trees seem to straighten
release and grow
and we are buried then, scattered in ash and bone
under the wind chimes,
waiting.

The Wind

My windows rattle and the trees list and crash.
The dog's ruff parts and he looks startled.
The wind tears down everything, demands
attention. She takes our breath and words
and casts the dog's barking far away, lost
in the swirl of sound that is the wind and not.
Every little thing has been reduced to this.
The temptation is to expect to find our feet,
to assert the bottom of this fear, a false floor
where we are momentarily safe. The wind,
seen and not seen, an ancient riddle
blowing death through the glass,
the jambs flex, cave and ache,
and a trickle of gooseflesh rises.

Bone by Bone

Lately I'm the Dilettante of Death.
Not a page turns or a show goes to commercials
that I haven't noted the death ride contained.
It's always there, the primary plot line, something
or someone is dying.

I used to say that I kept the tally
the master list, your karmic scorecard,
a run up to registering for the final class,
but I was deceived as the smart ones often are,
it's so much more simple than all of that.

Never mind, you'd like to say,
but even you know I am right. It's with us,
it has been in our bones since the beginning cry,
the beginning of need. Now it's just a countdown,
and we're shocked at the callous reminders

everywhere we look Death has the upper hand,
the glaciers melt, we walk across the shingle of beach
and can almost see the water rising, and we want
not to step back. We have failed. It is Time
that has the upper hand.

Smile and dance with me,
I am the Dilettante of Death, it rides
me like a war horse to battle,
bone by bone, flying in a
western wind.

Storm

This wicked wind, a ghost
with wings rapid, rattling, trapped
she is, between the window and the screen—
then a door slams somewhere else,
and the jambs and braces balk and murmur.

She builds an elusive energy,
an unbalancing, playing in the doorways
bending the window glass. And we wonder
what of the bird's nests? Are the chicks
tumbling, feathers and sticks and last sighs only?

Inside my skin, my gut, something also jumps
and jitters, there is no balm for this, somewhere
someone can explain it away with a barometer,
not here, not with the ancients bending,
and the weather vane awhirl.

Deadheading

I never do this. Blooms stay on the hydrangea
their blue, brighter than life itself, pales over the months of fall,
papering dry like old skin thinly veined, until some inner charge,
death's descant prodding, touches off the sweet budding:
sturdy little nipples pair each green stem
like a young girl in small clothes who stands confident
beside the matronly widow in her old fashioned hat.

And I think, this is life now.
Digging fingers into a shoal of wet black dirt.
Scattering seeds that nature herself has dried in my absence,
henbane's bells with thousands of opportunities for death.
Where shall I put them?
I don't have a plan,
I'm just wandering this wet dreadful garden,
scorning the riled up roses blooming out of turn,
wanting desperately to cut, censor, refuse.
Is this why the old lady gardens?

Cekes

I imagine these lines between us,
heart tethers, they flex and strand long, so long
from you to me, us to them, from above to here,
from here to below.
From the stars we have chosen,
the sweet spidery cord is a stairway
and we gather up the bonds that connect us like rays of the sun
and walk the constellation that is this startling path.
I imagine my heart without you,
bereft of some particular strength:
the one that makes me awake to the world,
the one that sees words
as beacons.
What makes us partners is the way in which our hearts duplicate,
the rare knowing measure that requires no retelling, no refolding.
You know what I know, there, down along the line
where beloved is One.

Cekes \'sē-kēs\ are the invisible connecting lines that the Inka
believe run between sacred power sights all over the world.

Conversation 1 — With Myself

How shall I talk to you now
now that gold and silver charms, blank with sparkling jewels
need to speak with an urgency we do not yet fathom,
hang still waiting for the right words. Now that everything
must have a purpose or be abandoned at the cliff edge.

Now that I stand at the edge I must look down
do you see? There is no other direction
for we are gravitational beings
and we have already taken the first step,
felt the whooshing sensation of life streaming away
our displacement already beginning.

I'm not uncomfortable with the Fool's cap
the pointed slipper, the long brocaded shroud;
but you see, don't you, that the charms arc around you
waiting. Waiting
and as I am falling so I am also reaching
snatching a word here of love, a word there
of strength, catching any hint of new ground
though none is there, you know that too.

I'm falling because I have jumped,
determined to see what I must remember for the next time,
formulate the future response,
cloud myself in the safety net of words.
That last sensation of feet on earth, of toes gripping,
what is so precious about that? Think about flight
the faller with wings, no fear.

On my back I can see that lopsided cross of stars
just above tree line now an arrow guided to my heart.
All of the mountains contain my dreaming
there is no fear you will ever forget.
But what is the story we must remember
before life is normal again?

Waiting to Thrive

In a two legged wobble dance
singular forms drift, conjure, and drift
out of reach on a winding path, a Fool's road.
I am waiting to thrive.

And while I wait there are things to do—
craft a Zen garden in the cat box, admiring
the way the gray pebbles clay, sucking life;
as if I might stick my thumb into it and come
away wizened, it would be that simple.

I am waiting to thrive, survive
nights of wanting to lie deep in the bath
so warm and let blood drain.
I would not care how bad I look in red,
but you would.

You are also waiting for me,
tender and whole, and the biggest gift
you have given is your offer to join this misery;
in surprise, we sat together on the bed
waiting to thrive.

Who are you to judge?

I am everything. I am the seer,
no thing alone will make the leap,
the magic key accessing the lock,
without first I release it from my sight.
I am the hummingbird's beak dripping with sap
waiting for flowers in a March wind
making do, marking time, seen

and unseen in a complicated contemplation,
a forest of words judged final.
The moment of release,
the word formed in a soft oval mouth,
the small exhalation for two or three syllables,
like the j-stroke arc of the little bright bird,
swift and suddenly gone. This life,

who are you to judge,
afternoons of sleep like floating
while the world rushes by beneath,
one long violent river, no bed for rest
no heart left for futures. Shrouds of regret,
bright colorful flags of ifs and worries
tied to a holy tree, a hawthorn,
taking blood or bond—my choice

and that's it, isn't it? My choice.
Who are you to judge? I am
everything. I am the seer,
left to my own internal courtroom
to explain, to say that not much happened
in this fragile life but waiting,
waiting for flowers in a March wind.

Palimpsest

When the news is bad
we layer up protection—a sandwich
of care overlaying the hurt and pain of disappointing
truths until we are left in a cocoon of non-doing,
a crackled glaze of all the emotions that came—
a sudden cascade—that day last fall
when the journey stopped for me, and the world
moved on.

Left within an egg of fear, questions as old and ancient
as stone remain unanswered. Like the fertile egg,
there is the merest moment between beating life
and the sustenance of death. No answers, no surety
as to the rightness of that dark hour. We will
all come to it, shedding layers, rewriting
while there is still time, scrubbing the parchment
clean in order to present a new face, a new moment,
scribing a palimpsest of the life we would have wanted.

This Business of Misery

As seductive as chocolate smeared sex
we are hippos, wallowing in our sense of self
and too often, too often it comes down to this,
this business of misery,

a catalog of barbs and trials
we have squirreled in our gut
ready to produce should anyone dare suggest
we have it made.

No, I said, I've never had my heart broken.
Instead of being a lovely thing, I needed to defend
such a shocking circumstance by adding, poor me,
that perhaps it was only I was never in love before,

now, the point is to rise above the calamity of aging
but not so far as to tempt Death. If we hang on to life
as a point to point rally of doctors' visits and tea time purgings,
sharing secrets and recipes in a malicious and viral glee,

what have we done with Life?
That graceful bird of anticipation,
like the moment just before your lips bend to my breast,
even scarred as it is, you bend, and I am full of joy.

Portal

Within your crease
the ocean pulses a regular cadence of froth;
and now and then a surge cleans the sand from
your inner membrane, slick rocks.

One by one we approach at ebbing tide
a single stone a simple prayer
mamacocha, sweet mother ocean
sweep us clean of care

and like a woman in full power,
no young thing, your wave surge comes
pulling at our feet, a staggering reminder
we are only a small thing, a simple shell

an empty casting of sand
waiting.

Darwin and the Dead Moose

Having just read that moose will grieve—
that therefore, there is a memory of mothering
in all living things—we have to agree now
that there is no such thing as instantaneous
death. The mother moose returns
day after day to the spot on the highway
where her little one last lay, what lament
does her heartbeat play?

She only gives up when the snows come
and she must move on, or herself die.

Now that we are forced
to admit we cannot frame superiority
out of human emotions, it seems that tenuous line
—slung out like a fly fisherman's easy cast—
that kept our hearts from breaking with every
turn in the road, that delicate line has snapped.
Now there are too many tears to shed,
and we cannot see to drive.

Making Pie

It may be that our joined expression of sadness is,
as it sits, a vessel we fill with these small petals of joy;
and we do not mind these sad tinges—a mud colored exhaust—
as if the dye of this lifetime were not fast,
and so we take our joys as tiny heart cracks, being
now and then too full of tears to venture much speech.

Together we lay the lattice crust
weaving another shared experience,
and someday we will look back
on the warm kitchen and the conundrum that is Nietzsche,
and remember how we learned
the scent of blueberries in this new way.

Conversation 3 — With Myself

This dawn is a self contained voice.
No anticipatory chatter, no tide of shafted light,
the fog that has dripped as if rain had come and gone
encloses us in brief moments of mute and pale
expectation. A chill and quiet stillness
broken only by ocean pulse and
the distant call of the lighthouse.

Contained in this voice
is a little silent advice: wherever
you are, begin, not as you would
a scrubbed and wrapped present
but just as you were the moment
you first heard the waves, new and naked
from sleep's grasp, from that time where genius lies.

Don't wipe, or cook, or drink away the words,
don't tuck them back into their darkness, turn,
face the dawn with all words tumbling,
open the door and cast them down the steps
out onto the brown weeds and red bricks
of your little life. Let them fall
let them fall.

Let the Rain Fall

Let the rain fall—
let the mother drink her fill,
wash the breasts of mountains,
make her milk run clear.

Let the rain fall—
and down the path of forgiveness
I'll put my face to the fog
and drench in the saddest knowledge.

Let the rain fall—
and from the juice of half a moon somewhere
up above the murk and glow, listen
listen to each drop, catch each dip and blush of flower,

Let the rain fall—
quiet the sodden animals, shepherd the lost,
these are only the candles the Muse lights
when she cannot talk to us any other way.

Graylag

The sweet sorrow of a voice
that never strays from minor key—a kindred range—
we are betrayed by the simplest speech.
Words we pick gently from a closed heart,
they make the listener strain to hear. Careful words
sung out of considered silence, and
as often as not, they bewilder and bewitch.
They create questions, a flight of seeking, of dismay,
like the partnered graylag, we know that loss,
the gunshot, the spiral, the lover lost.

Elegy for Faith

In the midnight hour, when the world's beauty is in the stars
we hold vigil with candles lit and watch in awe
as you make the journey across the milky way;
and we are grateful to you, not only for the gifts
of this life, but also because you have agreed
to go before us, to seek the bridge, and in going too soon
we have filled our hearts with you and will never lose sight
of you, never let you fade from our dreams. Sleep,
and seek the star that burns brightest for you alone
for there is one, and we will meet you there,
down along the way of all living things—
be soft now, be loved, be faith.

She Said

Because we are not dualists, we don't know who we are.
She would like an orderly informed progression,
something like her garden: a nursery of tenderness
the idea of succulent colors and an anticipation of taste,
that when growing fills her with energy,
like an orgasm for late age beauties. She mourns
the moment of peak, and with winter—
itself a shroud she would rather not wear—
she dies, wishing she knew then what she knows
and finding that now, she knows not herself
nor why it should matter.
Because we are not dualists, we cannot stand
in the path of life and off to the side observing.
We are either alive and agnostic or a ghost watching.
Sometimes we sense this ghost within us, trying to inform.
But in our haste we spill all of our lifeblood into the growing,
like the flowers in her garden, never knowing
the other side of balance.

As if by Magic

Magic is the circular route of our longing,
the keys that come unbidden
yet take precedence.
Magic makes the lifeline on your palm quiver,
realign.

As if by magic we are full
and then empty of promise,
we are satisfied and then yearning
for what we fear
we have avoided.
We are satiated and yet
our thirst could be no greater.

As if by magic, by the wind
whipping away our tears,
like the moment of skidding freedom
as the car turns and floats freely over the pavement.
As if by magic, all may be lost or gained in an instant,
it is your call.

A Spring Heart

Love is not a heart laid bare. No ocean
washes over us tangled in the sand. No doves
echo our secret words, no beating breast
matches the pulse of a strong and fully lived self.

Love is a soft safe corner, a warm flow,
a bath of scented elixir. Love is the way candlelight
makes us look beautiful. Love is not my heart
opened for you to see.

Love is one thought shared by two
not spoken aloud. It is gentle fingers'
exacting touch, just right in moment and
in purpose, a wealth of all care concentrated

into one sweet movement
when all is well again, love is whole and
unbound, the perfect timbre of those words
unsaid, a wise and soft smile lifting.

Resolution

A wandering path that turns back on itself, like the knot that
    anchors our hearts.
A guide, an essential arrow notched in a tree, long forgotten.
The descending notes of plainchant,
their final echo calling us to god.
There is only one true resolution, Death,
but it is such a little thing
in a universe so wide with souls in flight. Love life.
Be full with Earth joy.
Reach through the veil, seek the delicate jewel that is yours.

September Rain

The first rain is like a sigh, an exhale,
as if we have collectively held our breath in
one universal yoga pose of hope and longing,
waiting out the summer.

It begins always in the night, on a gibbous moon,
at the deepest moment of silence, no rustling
no flutter of settling birds, no furtive allies on the dirt below.
The ocean quiets herself, and the gentle cleansing begins.

This time, all night the gentleness came
with long minutes of
simple pleasure under an open window,
tucked beneath supple cottons,
revealing the depths and wonder of the healing needed.
And then sleep,
with storied oracles tugging at me, calling, and calling.

There should be a new word for the rain god of healing.
She is silk and cool dreams. She is a reason to stay asleep,
stay asleep and heal. Let the old wounds find their rest.
Walk the banishing way, put the day's work aside,
let the rain come calling.

Extremities

I'm not speaking
of hands and feet.
I'm talking about the other faces—
the briefest side view in the mirror
a fleeting sylph, a blur,
a whimper of advice or caution
dancing down my spine.
Some days these creatures are all I see.
They are the doubters, the screamers.
They categorize, summarize,
scarify and malinger.
Some days I make no progress
but float in the wake of an old moon, blooded
extremes, flushed and edgy.

The mirror reflects their gloomy leave-taking.
Waiting for their return
is to wallow in a feast of self sex and bad novels.
Waiting for extremities:
the wisdom keepers, wise ones,
angels and muse,
the ones who patter back and forth
across my mind
like bedroom slippers for an aged brain.

Holding Still

Is there a limit to stillness?
Sometimes the trees are an absolute of quiet inertia,
as if the Mother tugged at their roots in reprimand
for all the back and forth
the sway and wail.
She says rest, and all is quiet.

The ocean acquiesces with a glossy pattern
a reflection of unruly clouds
who won't stop for anything,
even the Mother.

Fog creeps within the trees
kissing gently here and there,
a capricious lover, a young one,
darting, curling. A sprite's logic.

Still there is absolute quiet
in the oaks, the pines, the elder fir:
Holding still for mourning
doves.

Birthday Greetings

In the pool in weightless grace,
the deep caress of water, my earth,
I can stretch into a false pose of soundless effort, my hands
slip over my tightening skull through thinned hair
trailing.
How small I am,
a collection of matter,
moisture and enlivened cell
shrinking.
Words escape within in a mist,
ramble around like bees do
their bone hive.
It used to be hard to clear the mind.

December

This is the time of long shadows
a shining path of stillness.
There is truth in the way of dying
that we, like the tiger, can eat
or be eaten:
we can think in death
or live in life.
For what is death but the undressing
unveiling disintegrating of sinew, blood and bone
for a freshening, an opportunity, a cleansing,
a renewal.

We can use logic to embrace this gift of mortality.
But, please, when I'm gone
don't tell my dog that I am dead.

This Fog

This fog doesn't come in on *little cat feet*,
it roils up the gulch like smoke
from a chimney in hell, snaps
its tail around the reed grass clinging
and sheers away, the way the buzzards arc
riding its invisible hand.

This fog is a long fingered lure,
come down, come down,
I'll help you, as the road bends and cants
and wind blinds your sight,
the old house no shelter, a witch
of battered boards, cold and abandoned.

This fog chases you, dives
and loops through the massive trees
pushes here, pulls there, arranges itself
a veil. No amount of rubbing will clear your eyes.
A siren fog, a chill cloak, where birds go silent
and the ocean licks her lips.

I See Winter

Unspeakable beauty.
I am beginning to know what that means:
around my heart ice forms
breaks, and forms again,
a cascade of emotion attached
to this winter world.
And then these mountains—
the sun steps across them
warming, begging, melting, demanding.

We are so very small.

What is it we will do with our truths?
I am still in quiet, cold shade,
but she approaches now,
crawls across the ridge line—
mountain and heart.
This is what I got up for, only this,
and it is enough.

I see winter
everywhere. The sadness has spread
and my shadow is what remains.
Unspeakable beauty, these mountains,
etched upon my broken heart.

It will be another day of adjusting.

The distant mountain path does not beckon.
There is this impulse in us for harshness,
discord that is the human condition.
Even on her surface
the lines scry
and lead nowhere
or a place I cannot go.

Singing alone is difficult work.

The mountainside ripples
as if she shuddered with ecstasy.
This icy winter
might require more than gods;
and my place in it
might not see her thaw
into that unspeakable beauty
we so long for.

The Bride of Quiet

What I know is that love is not enough.
Ruthless time mimics my static spaces.
It seems I can rummage around now in a brain copious
with furniture bare rooms, words
pattening on tiles, all echoes,
A vast cellular desert of spacious opportunity.

Where once were caverns—tight-packed spaces
filled with the magnificence of lived words,
now are dance halls laid gray and noisy,
as I, the bride of some quiet muse
struggle against the simple urge
of sleep.

Sloughing

In the same way that we are here in the last pages of my journal,
the whole may now be redundant:
so many cards chosen and repeated, yet still
The Fool stands
her cloak whispering the precipice,
her familiar a distraction not a guide.

In the same way disappointment reappears
like a moon time shadow, a Queen demanding blood,
the thread that made mere words something important
has stretched out into endless waiting,
so that its severing is a sloughing—
inside, torn, bloodied where we monthly recreate.
How many pieces of myself are there to lose?

In the same way that the oyster covets her pearl,
a speck of dust that became a glistening idea,
I dared to believe in wisdom.
Sloughing. Eventually we are dry,
our blood gone.
Embittered we recalculate losses
and reassign blame. Having learned nothing,
retained nothing, we forget to look for the link
between the glow of the moon and the pearl.

Maybe I'm Not Rapunzel

Maybe I'm not Rapunzel,
maybe I'm up here in the tower for a reason. Did you ever think
for one minute I might have a purpose? I might
long for this solitude, this well-spring deep in the stacks:
a library of tiny people my muse parades by for my consideration
crowd in here with me until I might just leap for it.

Or, I could let down my hair, now just a fond memory
but I still remember how you loved to ride it, and you
still remember otherwise you wouldn't caress me that way
those days I do come down; come down
and we make some conversation, two or three words is all,
and a touch.

And then I'm up here again with the gang
have you never heard such pestering?
Completely unsympathetic wonderings, the Little Dears,
there are no excuses up here, I'm waiting for No One. Go on
then and don't be so fearful, I can see the wind from here
and She speaks for all of us.

In Fire's Doorway

You can imagine the kaleidoscope, it will be
a brightness sharp as shards of glass,
the painful joy of knowing the one thing

the only thing left to know
is deep within, a tender shoot of sacredness,
not of words but of connections

knowing the one thing
is to step into fire's doorway,
speak with angels and have no one to tell

for truths are a human frailty
the gods don't care,
the only thing left to know is you.

The Summer Grandfather

I remember the sweet musk of cherry bark tobacco on his collar,
the shoulders hunched and the hip canted
a cigarette on its own attached to one dry lip the long ash
curving,
the tinkling of his signet ring
against the stubby Waterford whiskey glass—his crucible.

I can hear the deep resonance of a poet's voice, a voice
of someone who knows the command of his own words
the recitations *Abu Ben Adhem, may his tribe increase*
I didn't inherit that gift, can't recall a single phrase from memory.

I can smell the simple evening cake baking in the oven,
our bedtime snack long after
the moldy smell of public foyer tiles
and the echo of my steps as we intrude, long after
the excitement of Sunday best and Vaselined shoes,
one, two and three drinks later, dinner come and gone,
and now the best part, the simple cake,
just us and him, the bakers.

Years later, after the women are gone
and life is irrevocably changed by death,
I can feel the dock boards reaching
out into the calm northern lake
yield to my steps as I squat like a child at the edge
and I can hear him again, soft at my shoulder,
apologize for the immensity of his love.

Navarro with Dogs

Runnels of sodden sand,
a wet Sahara of river flow balloons
at the headland. Runoff is a peculiar word
for this swift flow of destruction.
Logs and tangles of drift
knit with foam and weed
as if the ocean opened her mouth
and foamed at us in angry purge.
Exhausted harbor seals beach out of reach.
We wander an erratic line of our separate selves
cordoned off by wind-tears
each of us lost within the scents of remembering.

Lake Storm

The wind shifts and the leaves of the broad maple turn over,
maidens offering themselves to the rain god, they stir and shiver
as the air becomes a power we can see.
The sky to the north, for here
change always comes from the north,
has become an ominous and
luminous blue cloud that dips into the water
of the farthest edge of lake shore.

We are sitting on the bank,
bare legs cooling in the dark soil and leafy detritus
of the water's edge. Our faces are sunburned, but now we are cool,
even chilled, as the temperature takes a dramatic turn,
and the water before us begins a gray dance
and we can no longer search for agates
in the softness of the shoreline.

Lightning, faint thunder, far off,
and like children we begin to count the seconds in our heads
between the flash and the rumble.
The boat tied to the dock
begins to duck against the piling in a following rhythm,
as a tempo builds and our anticipation rises.

The best ones rise with a fierceness
that makes us know how small we are,
the air crackles
and the rain holds off long enough for us to watch the storm—
watch as it walks across the water of the lake,
chasing loons and ducks
and fishermen until she owns this body of water
and she will do what she will.

The best storms come with eerie light of pale yellow,
and thunder that makes the china jump.

And when the rain comes it bathes the leaves
drenches the dusty paths and fills the boat at the dock.
We retreat, but sit inside without electricity
so that we can see the lightning, watch the wind dance
and whirl across the water,
and comfort the dog who doesn't have this relationship
with Llappa, the god of lightning and thunder.

Lie Back

Fear is the flutter of bird wings just out of reach,
random chatter.
What you want most is to take the white softness to your slack
    mouth,
muffle the cry your heart makes at the moment of rending. Pillow
deep in a quilt of dreaming days.

Deep in a quilt of dreaming days
aloft like an angel must be just at ascension,
lie back,
lie back and inhale the whiteness of freedom.
Exhale the long bardic chant: the secret known and forgotten.

Exhale the long bardic chant: an ancient tongue you
no longer recognize, the wind
licking your earlobe.
Lie back, dream of the fire you will come to before long.
For now, today loves you,
and that is enough.

After the Thunder There Is Nothing

I hear the rain
her steps across the dry grasses
a tender approach
from there, and there, and there,
fat summer drops, tears
cast across weathered boards.

After the thunder
there is nothing but the hermit thrush
and her constant song
as if no lightning had illumined her,
nothing but the wail of the Albion buoy
good...good....good, it says.

Thunder is my heart's food.
No gentle tug is needed here,
rattle my heart in its cage of aging bone,
strike close by and shatter the calm,
make me shudder
make me reel.

After the thunder, there is no thing.
The air, once compressed, relaxes her grasp
on a gentle wind
as if to sigh in rain
or exhaustion
at a heart so shorn.

Without a direct strike, her temper will pass us by,
we purse our lips and look, seeking the fire aloft,
but after the thunder
there is nothing.
Nothing but the sadness of a brief and elusive body.
No thing but a broken heart.

Global Warning

What does it mean
when the leaves blow from the West on midsummer?
When the lichen calls and I can hear the evening growth?
What does it mean when the mourning doves weep
and evening seems only to muffle their sound,
as the wind lasts too long into the night.
I relearn that precious things are mine for others to seek, to throw
a beacon of our histories, a long warm night of coverings,
like a gauntlet passed.
It is for me to bury them so that they may be found,
so far down the spiral,
a lineage of hide and seek.
What does it mean when the bright death of autumn
struggles to bleed past the rend of chain saws
but cannot?

The Summer of No Summer

This is the summer of no summer.
Stacks of pages, clean, bright, and crisp edge away
and preserve their virginity as if the taunting virgin
knows the whore inside too well.

Frittering, procrastinating, mindless musing
these are the occupations of a slack bodied mind,
rearranging furniture in hopes of finding truths
tucked in the seams.
This is the summer of no summer.

A relentless wind comes down from the North
as if from a god and sweeps all energy off like a desert blow,
while the flowers in the garden hold on and refuse to bloom.
Keep the coat on the banister, this is no summer, they say.

This summer is contained chaos, within and without,
dead birds piling up on an oily shore
each one counting a year of what is left to come,
No summer for them, no summer for us.

Gray skies and an unblooming garden,
who will be the first to go? Then the earth herself shivers
from the lack of warmth, of care,
and declares for all who wish to hear:
This is the summer of no summer.

The Owl

The owl is hanging upsidedown.
Sometimes superstition runs amok, a torch bearing
naked thing, chaos is his middle name.
Our job at the edge is to refine the string of logic,
it's not a wild flailing jump-rope, gaping, gnashing at our toes.
It's the most perfect of patterns never repeated more than once,
a prime fine looping line that fills out our bones so that we may
hang gold rings and crosses and superstitious charms,
so that protected becomes our middle name.

We can bury our pretty heads in iconography, hagiography,
call down the heavens
and move only from the lines of a newspaper star chart,
or we can find power in the one true still center,
the one deep within.
Core deep. The center where a lie lights a silver fire,
where truth is ever on trial.
Where all your thoughts are corrected for once
and for all. The owl is hanging upsidedown,
and it only means this: the housekeeper has been here again.

Planting

White and light as faeries, these fall seeds drift and spin
like some of my prospects, searching for a meeting place.
Like me, they look forward to the winter of dormancy,
where delicate notions can test their ground, the idea
of rootedness still only a promise that might not be kept.

Thistle seed seems always to just be passing by,
while acorns plummet headlong into whatever might be below.
Between these two, between Scotland and California, I rise
and search about the night sky for the right and single cast,
for the one thing that brings me to this equinoctial line:

not promise, not impulse, not compromise
only the one thing that will suffice: to be here now
and want no other moment.

Heart's Ease

This is a longing as large as love.
A strand of our genetic code, back and back
back to our place at the great fire,
the storyteller's circle, where we learned the tale,
the lineage of our tethering.

We want to know our place,
so that when we look into the great starry sky
we feel the perfectness of position,
as if the entire universe held us with a single silver strand.
We want to sit at the feet of the moon
and feel the earth cup our buttocks in dark, moist, soil
and know this place, my place.

Where have you wandered, sweet people?
Why have you strayed so far?
Do not sit idle, eyes closed. Open,
grasp the thin line of your belonging,
reach, leap, fly, regenerate, rerememember,
we are nothing without the mother, our earth

nothing without the stillness, her gift,
nothing without the depth of field.
Think back with your sacred mind, back
to the fire time, when earth was clean of us,
heart's ease is for every creature—bring it down upon you
bring it down upon us, one and all.

Anthropomorphizing, Again

I've got this relationship with a woodpecker,
every day he bangs his head against a dying bull pine
and, later, I suppose while he is away home nursing a headache,
all the little twittery birds come and eat beetles and decorate their
  beaks with sap.
He comes when I am watching, a flash of white, a jet of red,
he's not a grand pileated fellow, he's just a regular joe of a bird
considering the flamboyance of his kind;
but we have a relationship, I'm sure of that much,
and you know what it means as well as I
to be a bird on a dying tree digging for bugs in a hail storm.

A Bird's Life

Today like every other day
We wake up empty and scared. (Rumi)

Counting soft bellied quail skittering down
the summerhouse path, their elders live a life of
sustained panic, and though there seem still
to be perhaps forty of the young ones, I
am afraid to count. All I can do is leave the grass
long and brown, and have a care the dogs stay asleep
warm and sated in the noon sun.
And in the night, when cats, big and small,
follow a scent marked path under my window,
I hope the quail sleep, hearts beating fast and strong.

The evidence of the thread
this thread of delicate fates
brings closer, ever closer, the frailty of our lives;
and like the quail, we call and scatter
and reconnect
the energetic self,
fragmented with fear
of the one thing, the one thing bigger than ourselves.

An Anticipation of Gulls

On the lip of the ocean
a thousand gulls sit the prayer of anticipation,
their soft hearts count the waves.
What oracle tells them of the storm none of us can see?
What instinct turns their eyes, beaks, and bodies north,
bracing, a collective decision, a momentary calling to order
interrupting the scrawl and cry and flightful chaos of bird life.

An anticipation of gulls, we slow to watch, the curving inlet
at the little river a towering but momentary shelter.
Later, the ocean will throw her will at them,
scatter them with the thud of logs
and crashing waves laden with sand and stone.
But now they are a warning,
unanimous in their attention, all arguing at bay.
And we watch the sky grow dark with wonder,
simple primitive selves,
hoping for a gale.

Death of the Dove

I want to hear the mourning dove
pronounce the word fidelity—for you, for you you you.
Even though she is nearby
still he calls and calls
his voice is her tether.

Like you and me, the doves ride tandem trees,
his branches are broad, bare and mossy,
yours are strong and clear.
Her branches are leafed and trembling,
mine are delicately narrow and reaching.

I want to hear the mourning dove
and while I'm weeping for the death of a pair
while the feathers still flutter to the ground
and the hawk is satisfied,

I wonder what will you do
what will I do
when our tether draws tight, snaps
and one of us is left, mourning,
watching the hawk withdraw.

Drift

The night sky bows a brief performance
conceding an early victory to the small birds of dawn:
the hermit thrush in joyful heralding, an urgent awakening.
I always think of Rumi now, at the dawn,
but I never do stay awake, choosing instead to lie quietly,
the cool breeze drying the perspiration of thick sleep,
contemplating which dream to return to,
and how I want it to end.

One Hundred Crows

I live in a house surrounded by elderberry that will not bear fruit.
I walk the angles and beg to no avail,
for once they have determined
this is not their zone in any season,
they go about their hapless growing
like I go about flinging words onto pages
with no audience bearing the pains of my poor delivery.

Down the road there is a stretch of green
cut through by an old fashioned draw
where I see ghosts of sheep hobbled
and dying in the muck of that envelope,
while one hundred crows play a tune drumming and piping
and dance the dance of death and delight.

They dance death for us all
though they are fond of lamb in particular
and however they glean the insight
they seem to know the door has opened long before we do.
We are listening with the wrong frequency.

I live in a house surrounded by elderberry.
They push new growth in spring,
green on green, on green, against every window
and I think, surely, a berry, even once.
There is salt on my altar and crystals at the corners
but still the omens are not encouraging.
Even a mated pair of crows is still crow medicine, you see,
warning me not to take heart,
not to take anything not rightfully my own
but death when She comes.

One hundred crows is not a hand I can beat,
no matter how many queens are involved.
One hundred crows, a mass mourning ritual

so arresting I pull off the road to wait
for blood & display, flight & ignition.
I wait for the inspiration that comes
like their stark and black beating wings.

I live in a house surrounded by elderberry,
drinking old fashioned nectar out of the night moon.
The finite elements of walls, window glass,
rails and gritted clapboards
are the pegs upon which I rest my words:
shiny little frailties that come down like heaven,
followed closely by chaos.
We are all tender without fruit,
the product of denial, desirous of warmth and picking.

Three Blue Herons

Three Blue Herons ladder up a skeletal tree,
bare branches all darkness shanked with green usnea;
a perfect perch for three old crones drying, watchful,
minding the river flow below.

It's time, they say, have no fear. Every single one of us
comes to this moment by themselves. Embrace
the passage of time with a soaring great stroke—
with your best cast, your most perfect strike.

Be it maiden, mother, or crone take the wind
beneath your body and find the warm current—
the one with your name on it, written
with the ink of a thousand deaths before.

Strip the covenant of your vanity and look hard and deep,
for underneath lie the silver stars of the ageless sky,
the golden warmth of the sun god's gaze,
underneath at last, the depth of gaze in your blue eyes is

everything, the measure of all that might be
and has been, reduced to three paths,
three crowns, three birds who guard the gate.
Pick a life, and watch it flow right away, right away.

Great Horned Owls

We stood as the moon crested the shadowed dark of
the tall stand of pine and fir, still and gentle between us,
while there just above, two great owls
made love with their words
who, who, oh ah, who
their calls a give and take of urgency and promise.
And from every direction around us a concordance of owls
calling and calling on this full moon night, all of them roused.
Not yet in pairs they rise to some ancient urge and for hours
turn their faces to the moon. Now and then one moves,
perhaps to get closer to his desire, and the chorus shifts,
the calling juveniles trip over each other,
the booming voice of the female persists, demanding,
settling, as the pattern renews and builds.
And just as suddenly with the moon high, they are silent,
and I think, little mole, tiny rabbit, beware the appetite
of the prowling ones, and then I sleep, with the wisdom of owls
still cast about us in the dark.

Brown Pelican

The gulf sea, agitated and gray, still settles us,
the pelican and me,
into a cadence of energy, a rising…

a falling, and I imagine his great gullet
filling with the words I'm rolling around my mouth
not yet certain of their order or importance,

words that glimmer like the sun on the wave crest
words that run deeply like the fish he dearly wishes.
And now and then he carries my words up into the sky

banking, a flick of unsteady wing trembles, he hesitates
and dives, so certain, and I turn back to these strewn pages,
myself hoping for fish.

Elegy for the Season of the Woodpecker

The chill descends through pine boughs
bringing the winter sough and crackle—
delicate ragged branches of a tree that
probably, this year, will fall.
The lone red crested woodpecker vacated
yesterday, leaving his companion, a solitary
hummingbird to the last of the hardening sap.

I wonder, does this mean the work is done?
Does this mean that what will die will die,
what will fall away, fall away—a winter cleansing
as gale winds whip across this little forest of mine.
And, I expect, some words will fly away as well,
fly away, when winter brings her cold bones,
and plays a mourning tune.

Waiting on a Snag

Six slick black cormorants face south,
the river snag exposed for a time by tidal exhale.
They are still, long necks raised to the midday sun,
wings tucked, waiting.
Around the snag an arctic loon flips and dives
newly arrived, carefree with relief
and the silly joy of being on vacation.
But I'm with the cormorants, feeling greasy and stuck,
clock ticking, the tide rising, forcing my own
ebb and flow, wings not dry enough to fly.

Pelagic

Being of the open water of the sea
no bottom, out of any depth calculable,
the sea bird that lives on the surface of the vastness
needs no mooring, no resting place;

unhinged from great black skids of breeding ground
flying in pairs if they are lucky, away, far away beyond landfall
the great ocean birds bring wonder and fearsome respect.
Pelagic, this is what love is.

Empty Room

Think about the sound of an empty room,
your footsteps, an echo upon
worn and curved floorboards, longing
for the emotional furniture of our lives.
What is it that makes this life worth your pulse?
Walk into the room, the slanted winter light
through bare windows, sharding across scoured boards,
many lifetimes of floor and wall

the emotional furniture of your life,
what is it that you cannot live without?
What buffers the echo of an open room,
a door unhinged,
what tattered drape conceals your lust
your faults, your future?

The sound of an empty room,
small footsteps made large,
what can you bring to furnish your life?
How strong can you be on your own?
Where will you place the seat of your becoming?
Who will come to your sitting?
What is it that makes this life?

Some strong, strange features,
like the summer beam of the kitchen,
the narrow staircase, the shriven walls
the old house of my life is bare. Think
of the sound of an empty room,
of footsteps, an echo, a pathway,
a map of the journey laid bare.

Full Moon Woman

One. She. Fertile. Full.
Since when did these words become stones?
When did embodying the full female self
hang like a burdensome shame?
When did full pendulous breasts mean the goddess become worn?
Silent. Gone.
One. She. Fertile. Full.
We step away from the embrace of the moon in her prime
hoping our flesh will turn thin and sheer.
What do you become when you wear a zero?
When round is you empty? A pile of sticks, bones and blood.
One. She. Fertile. Full.
Who looks in the mirror and hopes for the great One? Belly full,
breasts smooth, more than you can hold,
mountains to the valley of pleasures.
Come down. Oh come down.
One. She. Fertile. Full.

One. She. Fertile. Full.
Bring you to me. Bring you now.
Let me wrap my legs around your needy self,
tight, a dark and easy pool.
Let me stretch and expand to hold your firmed flesh.
Bury, ah bury, like salt, sand and earth.
Come down, come down, until you have no choice.

Give me your animal, and weep.
One. She. Fertile. Full.

Hummingbird

This time the hummingbird at my window is lively,
fat and insistent,
not like before, so weary—a signal of separation—
he's back from his distant travels, flashing flame orange
and fungal green
as if he has been someplace exotic and eaten mango blossoms.

He's back, my harrying reminder
—the journey is long and sweet—
and as the wind of spring rises and we rouse our bear-selves
out of the storytelling time, away from the fire waning,
what equinoctial promise can we make?

While the earth floods her breast, her cyclic cleansing,
while she shakes free of the debris of human kind
hummingbird comes again, asks
and we follow.

Pileated Woodpecker

Because time has chaos as its middle name
and the path to the center of the earth is, indeed, a spiral,
the birds have sent the clear message, the bigger option,
and this ragged pine tree will bleed her amber essence
out to him, knowing we are at the edge.

Straight before me, all morning long,
so that there can be no doubt,
no question who this message is for,
no frittering delays, the pileated woodpecker,
king and master of relentlessness.

Work is the only option when time cracks
like a witchy mirror and you see all your various selves
chattered across a worn wooden frame.
And so I ask you, as I ask myself
what is your heart's work?

The Family Hawthorn

There is an encouragement of berries on the slender branches,
just a few, randomly placed. I hadn't noticed before this morning
but stopping on the landing, one hand on Buddha to seek
a moment of stillness, to arrest the progress of the day,
there in the window frame, six or seven red notions,
the first fruits, triumphant, like the child first born,
a particular and splendid gift.
They are all possibility and hope—tiny new leaves, narrow stalks,
almost more growth than those below can hold,
and yet we move forward, hoping for the sweetest in life,
welcoming the idea of expansion, of sharing the wealth of love
that grows strong and deep in our roots.

The family hawthorn, the tree of magic and heart power,
we propped it up with fence posts and fed it from spirit's source.
We watched as it ranged and shot and grew without thinking this
or that, and pruned it carefully now and then
in our usual random way.
It stands slim and gawky, competing with the houseline, as
we sit in the garden staring, imagining what it would be,
years beyond this life for us, someday a towering fierce tree.
But today, there are just berries,
a dozen hints of what might come,
a dozen sweet red bits of the possible,
just enough for this season of joy.

Two Ravens for Quinn

Thought and Memory,
their liege lord is the one who makes thunder;
he has made them clever and fearless.
As night pulls aside the covers to reveal
the sumptuous body of day, two ravens
wet behind the wing, circling
circling. Thought and memory,
we bind ourselves to this moment of birth;
hold our silence well,
deep in prayer, for nothing before
and nothing to come will ever match this dawn.
Two ravens, your guides, thought and memory—
I give them, give this, our lineage, on to you.

Perigee Moon

This near thing, a thin veil
the close shoreline of a known universe
pulling us in a tidal flow of conviction,
of a collective conscience, a moon
for a new age, no choices remain.

We have soiled her with our human step
aimed passed her toward the fiery one,
belittling the incontrovertible truth of a grave
and compelling ocean which waxes and wanes
and we think, oh, how lovely—

when really it is our limit,
our boundary, our death comes along
this round and pale glory smiling
in her perigee, kissing earth tonight
constant lover, she will come again.

Night Rider

It could have simply been the penumbral darkness of his cloak,
a gallantry of shadows, unfixed and momentary,
I thought it was love come riding.

There is such a thing as being too ready,
a lubricated sentience of the brain, overwrought:
grasping with the knuckled figures and quick tongue of witches.

Whatever it was, I could have stepped within its shadow,
swallowed its darkness—a whole cloth,
I would have wanted that.

Skinkling

Perhaps it's the narrow groove of a sharp turn
where roots invade the trail, or
a rare pale blue tail-less lizard,
known to cause death in the instant of its kiss.
No? Well, then, the tavern keeper in the act of pulling a short pint
might be closer to the truth, the root,

or, this, how I feel wandering empty rooms,
inside out, vast and space-less, without ground or level,
out of plumb and without heart, bloodied and witless.
Mean and meager, a dagger's slice
is skinkling, like death come unexpected, this is what is left.

Peonies

Like many things, like love itself,
they bloom too fast:
fat and fragrant, almost too much for their stems,
they reach and dip away from the green glass vase,
my grandfather's favorite,

like me—well loved, full, true pink petals,
they take me back to a warm and humid summer day,
a cool shaded hallway where, centered on the antique table,
an uncountable brilliance of peonies, their scent heavy in the air,
fainting with love.

Equinox

There is more than a spring cleaning needed here,
no simple rearrangement of furniture will do—
though it couldn't hurt—a voice says in the deep reaches,
to move this here, put that there, shake out, sweep, and survive
another week of rain and dim light. Cobwebbed
and crabbed within, there is little left to say, chiding,

forgiving oneself is harder than love.

Joy is love
uncluttered and unhampered by dread. Somehow
I must bring myself to that instinct, be a seeker of joy.
Light, dark, life, death, awake, and not, what we sow now
we will reap come June, the cock crows all day,

that's reason enough.

Mood

Everyone says there is no timetable for this.
Even so, I wake some mornings with resolve
and often goading, demanding that perhaps this day
will begin a new cycle. Now on a Sunday morning
mourning doves call in the hasty moments
between sun showers. And while the forest
still drips with tears, I can see progress in the clouds
as they move onshore and toward me,
knowing I am nothing special, this time,
on a planet with only a single moon for shadow.

Dream

I dreamed that horses could fly,
the key, they told me, was to stay on the clouds,
not the clouds we have in the west—thin and vaporous—
we want to ride the orange flames of cumulus at sunset
lightning zigzags beneath our hooves.
As the horse, I want the cushioning of the fullest cloud
carrying my brown belly and haunch, long legs dangling.
As rider I want to lay my body along her flank,
twine my hands in her dark mane, close my eyes
and let whatever will happen
happen. No more effort required than a single cloud
fully formed, and the right horse,
the one who knows she can fly.

64

The woodpecker started a new tree,
experimenting with the temper of the pine,
to start at the bottom, the top, or someplace in the middle,
that was his dilemma—
whether to start at all has not come into it, he knows
the work is there waiting for him every morning.

There is competition, does that drive him forward?
Or is one tree much like the next, living the life
of a driven state such as his, echoes of an ancient voice.
Every morning the forest seems dark and large,
as though there might be some part left untouched,
nascent.

We could call the days finished, stand aside,
let the pages fall, ink dry, a story skewed
in hapless energy, the kind of doubled bind
from which there is no happy ending
no escape. Some trials are not put down
for winning, some just are.

Máthair Críonna — Wise Mother

Grandmother Moon,
it seems you have taken it upon yourself to fill the void—
the one created by our striving,
to shelter us with your pale light, a quilt of calm.
You make us look more closely at the tiny cracks
the crevices, the shadows, this is the way of winter seeing.
You ask us to sit long into the night,
still and watching, a vigil to your passage.

And so I settle myself in the window, perched
over the forest of silence, hoping,
watching, holding the space between us
as sacred, alive. A quiet wondering
comes with each illumination, each grove in light,
as if you say, be calm,
watch beneath the surface
make the measure of your longing.

Be as the child in wonder
that the moon could come visiting the stairwell
shining, night beyond night, and no longer care why.
Just think about what it would be like
to lie naked drinking her light, the grassy earth your bed,
on a rowan moon in January, no tears to shed, nothing
needed at last but this simple self.

Grandmother moon, máthair críonna, mamakilla,
hold us gently sweet mother, hold us.

Part 3

New Poems

Outskirts

From my hesitant perch— say that old sinker log on the beach—
always on the outside of the crowd, the boundary of village
and villagers, seeing too far a distant horizon
searching the undergrowth of wave swells for whale spouts
searching for some comfort I can call.

Come to me, come to me,
it should be obvious that the line has been drawn,
meaning obscured, and yet still I want you here
sharing my fire, a ring on the outskirts, a low flame
kindled for spirit, not for heat.

Come to me, come to me,
I'm asking for your eyes not your smile,
for the long knowing, the gap bridged instead of growing.
We might be invisible but for our charms and graces;
some clan mother from the dream time spun from my cells, she calls

Come to me, come to me.
Dance at the outskirts, the crossroads, the brink, come
dance in the forest grove, at the fire's edge, the peak, come
dance alone, with the dogs, to the drum's beat, come
come to me, come to me
come to me sweet.

Let Go

Here is where it lies
it is the sharp edge of a mare's tail cloud
it is the horizon of the seventh league

at some moment, let go—

Emptying the mind
cling to the cliff
in the small rain-tempering wind

let go—

The side of this that is visible
is the imprint of a tattooed heart
a single name, a feral emotion

let go—

eyes closed, a darting star-filled galaxy world
the sense of air and the place beneath breath
weightlessness so close

let go—

a straight-line file body
relax,
where is your end point?

let go—

the shape of things to come:
no wishes, no tears, no pain
remain. Be clear thought.

let go—

Where is your edge, your silvery surface
where will you see a clear moment?
or is it after the whispering comes?

let go—

after the gathering in the grove
after the chanting echoes beyond new growth.
At the forest's edge now, step up

 let go—

Bend before the full fire of life
sleep upon the scabrous angry weed
burn as bright as you may and then

let go—

Count up your lifetimes, find the spaces between,
it is there that spirit lies
waiting, wanting

let go.

Cormorants

Congregationalists. Always
hanging about in a group,
occupying the snag
broad wings spread
praying to the sun.
Pelagic these are, I'm told
they hardly live up to their name:
perennially perched on dead trees
lofting omens all around
not out to sea
rather comfortably harnessed
to the ages of the river—
now a gentle flowing
but never out to sea,
with no need of snags.
Places we will never be.
In that case, they should be
atheists, or singular rationalists
certainly not dualists,
as above the water, so below.
Hang around and see.

Raccoon Tracks

Evening crossing the bridge,
the ducks are shadows
tracing a V line,
a last tour of their domain for the day
or are they looking for nestings?
I don't know these things, not yet.
In the darkest of the new moon night
Have they all come ashore,
some misbegotten lure
deep in the cycle of their gene pool
forgetting the fourfooted foe
the raccoon?

Friends

In my mind we have wandered
into a vivid green landscape mothered by a pale sky
that makes the eyes tear with its clever
patterns of cloudwhite: a wigged giant, a map of England,
a dusting from the faeries.
We climb across moss and heather with gentle steps,
boots wet with dew and tickled with grass,
our hems damp and welcome where they graze
against ankles bare. Now and then, often really,
we stop; sometimes you stop so that I can breathe
but you pretend it is for some flower, some small joy
hidden among the granite that floats on boggy ground.
Other times we sink together with a flood of captured words
upon startling a hare, and we wait patiently, sending her safety
and earth's love. Brown and sleek she eyes us and leads us
off her trail and we strain to gather her purpose.
Later, we open to a clean page and each of us tries to bring
her onto it, without much success, but she lends us the right words
and we make her into poetry lest her life not have enough
    consequence.
Now and again, you or I will read. Because of where we are, it will be
Wordsworth first, but others will follow.
And after we have read, and drawn,
and after we have poured the last cup of hot sweet tea from the
    thermos,
we will sit among the stones and let the wind tell of her journey,
wrapping us with a new lineage like a shawl of ancient madder
    thread,
as we learn even more of the story we already know.

Cottage Life

Even if you leave all windows open
east to west, still
there will be a dead tit
on the sill in the afternoon,
warm from the sun, and
perhaps from his way of life
the constant cautions around the feeder
greedy friends

or perhaps kitty finally decided
we deserved a treat
having trespassed as surely we have
her hedgerow to gate house manor.

Anyway, even if you leave the windows open,
while you drift near sleep watching
bumblebees over the pansied windowbox
and relish completeness of air
without window screens
still, someplace
a door will slam.

Late in the afternoon
we learn about ennui
as we carry chairs into the garden corner
looking for shade. We drink our tea
and figure out what to do
with leftover bread
knowing first we have to bury the bird.

Night Flying Woman

Deep in the body of a moonless night
I took my blood and flesh out for a spin.
Light and supple as fairy wind
I tested 'round the bedroom walls
and then fell and slipped
between the halls
off out, out into the darkness
the darkness of the night,
there watched by quiet birds,
observed and witnessed by the cat
I danced in white circles of skin and bone
and flew, a spray of stars and words
like a witch come alive
'round the dazzling fire.

Still Life in Winter

I don't have to remember a dimly recollected time,
something captured in sepia tones set to violins far away,
I look up from the page, the ocean distant, constant
and a doe wanders carefully across the path.
This is today, not the past of imagined safety,
this is a scar worn age.
There are too many dandelions to manage,
the stair-rail is rotted and pink with mold,
beyond effort, we hardly notice.
Slipped between seasons and suddenly
out of control, so that the doe needn't fear
doesn't see the path
for the detritus of a windy winter.
Birdsong and the sough of forest calm—
sentinels against the hungry ones. Me,
I'm in my chair too near the door,
waiting.

What is behind the door of this life?

How hard is it to stand when you have no ground?
When moon and sun set in unison,
when there is no bottom,
no false shelf of title-less books ready to swing wide
another safe room to fill
another stairway to downward darkness, only
a cold shelf of dusty music scores
and one dead grandmother left minding
a storehouse of women's memories, pointing deeper, deeper
a faulty light-switch bare bulb glow shining
too well on a single option.

What is behind the door of this life?
What is the secret we long to remember
only to forget again?
What is the difference between fate
and a life of wandering, between Fool and Wisdomkeeper,
when you have no ground, no ground,
only a mountain left for dreaming.

Summer

Clear slow water a shallows of rock and leaf,
a steep shore, wooden dock
a small boat tethered there, it moves
in rhythm with the water, knocking gently
on the pinion, it's an old launching not far out—
just short of the big tree, a water dragon—

By end of day we are burned golden
and scrubbed clean, lying by the fire
looking for aces in the grubby deck of cards,
an old worn cardigan and blistered feet.
They let me win, being the only girl
there were privileges and pains.

Cousins (For Jim)

Last night I dreamed we got married
like we always said in our six year old hearts we would.
Remember the blue plastic valentine?
I wonder what happened to that—
a precious object it traveled around the world in my pocket
just like you did.

Like the exactly stranded DNA that binds us
we spun out our own ways,
filled in the sameness between us, the trust,
with funny quirks and deep pieces of pain,
we grew both together and apart.
And this building that we each architect as our grown self
always had a doorway for the other and paths well used between us.

We could have been twins, instead we are cousins.
We could have been lovers, instead we are true friends, travelers,
we could have been the only dreamers in families of blindness,
but we were born together under the same constellation
and the story written by our meandering
is in a language only known to us.

I remember the day I realized we weren't identical,
the panic of the moment, thinking you were lost. There was a war
and you were gone in a way I could not follow or create from
    memory.
You grew up before me and ran off to prove it,
that and other things.
As usual, chaos reigned around you,
but you jimmy'd a space just safe enough.

So much later, because I knew I owed you this,
I made a place for you where you had always a right to come,
and together we found a new ground, fashioned from memories
and truths and pain

just in time to bury the Old One who loved us well
as one and as ourselves.

Last night I dreamed we got married
but of course, we are so far beyond that convention
that to dream it now is surely a simple sign,
a premonition. And I could just ask, but between us
words are only a small match to the fire of knowing.

And Then the Ravens

Early and late, a ruckus of ravens
a convocation business meeting
chapel of them at dawn
demanding I listen.
I push my head against the window screen
the light shifts through the trees
the sun not across the horizon,
their wings wet and sticky
from pine perches and slumbering,
a still fog, another veil
they cackle and squawk.
None of my business. They
hop away and then close ranks:
discuss, argue, resolve.
One flight, the chosen representative,
flies straight at me while the rest watch,
finally silent, decided. He lifts his body
inches from my face, wings wide
his belly soft and legs camped as he rises.
Got it? he says.

Counting Sheep (a pantoum)

Smoke dies away from the witch's cottage.
Fairies play hide and seek among the moss.
Yan Tan Tethera Fethera
counting sheep is an endless task.

Fairies play hide and seek.
An enchantment grows over me:
counting sheep is an endless task
spinning great trails of cloud born lies.

An enchantment grows over me
silky and sweet, eyes closed and weeping
spinning great trails of cloud born lies
the clans gather fiddling and pipe me to sleep.

Silky and sweet, eyes closed and weeping;
truths shatter and reform,
fevered bonds, invented shackles
counting sheep is an endless task:

the shepherd trusts his fingers
Smoke dies away from the witch's cottage
sleep, sleep, silky and sweet, eyes closed,
Yan Tan Tethera Fethera Pimp.

Advice

I want to tell you of all the things I've seen and done
the cascading free fall chaos of a life,
but all that seems important has yet to be

no thing I've seen or done is worth the telling,
the words would come too smoothly
shaped and formed with more care than cause.

No telling of the layering of feeling and fear
to see so often things prematurely
eyes not yet open for grace.

I want also to explain my worth:
create a ledger in slant lines, determine the ways
in which my hand is unique, justify this convocation of mind and
  memory.

I want to tell you all of the things I have seen and done,
an erasure for the wasted years, the servitude.
Collapse the good times into one prime numbered event

(nothing I see here equals that)
select for you the wheat of purpose
golden suns and silver moons.

Some galaxy of weeping waiting lives
threads a random collapse of warp & weft, a universe:
We insist on order, don't we?

I want to tell you so that you needn't go there.
Walk the singular walk through a thirsty fire,
webbed and waxing, small and caught.

Like a pale mare poorly harnessed,
these things for telling her soughing—
there is no point but to stand her ground—
no words for the telling, no sound.

Conversation 2 — With Myself

We don't know whether reincarnation exists
because who would want to carry forward, like a debt terminally
unpaid, the lives already lived? How cluttered and confused
each life would be, a muddle of anticipation and rue,
compensation and shadow, there would be no present.

I wonder, if when the living of all corporeal life is done,
and we reside at last in Being, if then we can recall
each life in its best moments — or worst — and
smugly look down upon a struggling world
and sigh.

The Three Wicked Sisters of Mortality

Nostalgia, Melancholy, and Imagination,
the three wicked sisters of Mortality,
taunt me with what might have been
if only I had been more brave.

Nostalgia dresses in cotton voile, finely tucked.
She whispers always, sometimes kisses a gentle leafy breeze of a kiss.
She brings little moments of tears while sipping tea, paging through
   old books.
She wants me to remember, enshrine, glorify.
She wants to see me bathing, floating in the clear and shallow water,
the long branch of the birch making a pattern on my breast,
eyes closed to the sun, care and careless, at one, a keepsake of mind.

Melancholy crawls in the closet with a blanket, defines today
by yesterday's hurts. Melancholy knows what that house transit
   means,
the one about 'open enemies and family'.
She cannot untangle the web of curses, unfold the story of sadness,
she cannot escape the cascade that is disappointment only humans
   throw.
She comes on like a black shroud, a moody ranting moon-tide
   witch, she
bites her tongue before she tastes the dark wine.

Imagination is what keeps her going, Mortality could stop by
leaving Death behind like an afterthought, but Imagination works
   her wiles
and usually leaves Miss M. outside anticipating the wonder.
Imagination invites the muse to pretend that anything is possible
(she keeps the knowledge that this isn't true to herself).
She barters for treats and keeps lists of the best of things.
She makes how you look in the mirror untrue, but easier to see,

the three wicked sisters of Mortality,
it's a crowded complicated bed in which we lie,
we are the sum of the triple, a multiple of worlds and times
not of our own making, responding and responsive,
tied and tying an inflow tide of stranded being,
it is a solo ride of triple faith, faltering before death comes:
three blood tide hags on the appointed day dancing the spiral dance.

Winter Sun

It is a clarity giving light.
Close your eyes and let the warm fire kiss your face
listen with an open palm to the soft measures of water:
river's edge a wavering line of lapping weed,
the coots chattering their welcome
bring in the winter sun,
remember how it comes,
and how soon it will go,
the soul memory of ancestral hearth-fires
temporal glow.

Banshee (a spell)

White voice of the Other,
howler from the heavens,
bender of trees, caller on the mountain,
now down my chimney
now through the cracks,
prize open the windows
seep beneath the door
moaning portend, wailing warning.
Banshee, March mother, wind warrior
High Priestess, Death Mistress, Singer of the Bones.
Firefall, blood bond, white Shewolf,
Stalker of the quiet world
bring it down, bring it down.

Waning Gibbous

Hunched like an old crone hanging over the winter garden
plucking the last bits of cordial leaves, now dark with rot,
—we used to call them old moons, by nature being negative—
a waning moon approaching rebirth, exhausted of her light,
I am

witched into the corner of the silver age of disappearance.
It's not a radical movement, just the incremental wizening
of one lifetime. No one said how much we would want,
how charged we have been by the moon in her current.
As if, by following her lead, we would find favor with greater gods,
but no

hunchbacked, gibbous, perhaps we simply cannot become
straight, the light too bright for bleary eyes. Instead we will gather
by the kindled fire, feeding dreams less than spellworthy
between the twigs and staves, and pass the cup of the wise ones
around us one more time, we've done all we could,
witched

flying now, the way we can, silverhaired and cackling,
and the only ones who think we're funny are the wee ones
who have no speech of their own, not yet. Soon enough,
soon enough we will fall silent and morose, and sit cornered,
chair bound and flightless, watching for a gibbous
moon on a waning curve.

Mortal (a villanelle)

Spring's smothering in rampant growth.
She pulls all my juice and leaves me dry.
I breathe, I sleep, fly far and softly in my dreams.

Waking late to fast light clouds,
pine boughs laden with vivid cone,
spring's smothering in rampant growth,

and I, I'm dying as surely as the Fall
desiccated, pale and weary, wintering;
I breathe, I sleep, fly far and softly in my dreams.

Earth's smallest particles cradle across the air
microscopic miasma of fruit and flower
spring's smothering in rampant growth.

My limbs are heavy, my head is numb
nothing beckons, nothing breaches, perhaps now I'm done.
I breathe, I sleep, fly far and softly in my dreams.

Here I sit while lilacs bloom, encased,
overwhelmed by potential and by doom.
Spring's smothering in rampant growth,
I breathe, I sleep, fly far and softly in my dreams.

Full Moon Coming Down

The full moon comes and places her head on my pillow,
and it's not a gentle sigh she gives as she lies next to me,
there is a cold rage leaking in the pure ice rays of her gaze,

as if she needs to scream but has no words.
Instead she brings up the tide and with the churn of water
hurls rocks and redwood across the sand,

and while the river is blocked
she's making up her mind where and what to create—
whose urges will she cause to overflow, whose anger will she
   swallow,

who comes to watch her nightly
bathe in her streaming light
who is the faithful follower? she asks me again

just as she asked the last time
she crept in beside my sleeping self
and took me in her arms to breathe heartbreak and rage;

and rage she will as long as we neglect the Grandmother,
her silver skeleton nothing good to sleep beside,
her bony embrace the cool ice of a million miles away.

She's coming down, silver streaming hairs of a restless tether
if only you could see it, but She knows well enough
that would be the Death of you. Full moon coming down, coming
   down,

full moon coming down.

Beltane (a villanelle)

Before we kindle the herald fire,
before we dance and kiss and slip away
let's pause in humble wonder at the gods

who let these winds so furious,
who split the ocean floor and surged
before we kindled the herald fire.

Before we drive the cattle down
before we decide whose lie is true
let's pause in humble wonder at the gods.

Who rails down upon us now?
Who will take the turning time
before we kindle the herald fire?

Before we drown beneath the mire
who will seek the spiral line?
Let's pause in humble wonder at the gods.

As chaos rains down and down, and blooms
no flowers soft, no colored spring.
Before we kindle the herald fire,
let's pause in humble wonder at the gods.

Conversation I

Speaking of the moon—
she had a ring around her when I first looked last evening,
I can't remember what the ring is called
or what it means but it was nice
a pale golden wedding band of completeness;

and then hours later, clear and white high in the sky,
she's such a nag, even sick she wants me up and thinking.

Conversation II

She said, 'You were probably hoping for something more ethereal.'
The ring around the moon, formed by ice
crystals in atmospheric surrender—
an invisible aerie binding spell, she casts
and I remember the first time I saw it, the ring,
years ago, and the tiny frisson of fear
that there is so much unknown, so much out of our grasp,
so much left before we go.
A spell of keeping still would be good now
one for noticing, remembering,
a litany for details so that every single aspect of that winter moon
will shine in my eyes long
long days after she has darkened once again.
In the rush for tomorrow, a spell for today is what I need, a hand,
a tether to keep me from lifting toward her
as she beams down upon us all.

Moon in the Twelfth House

and she's rising dark as they say
no shining guide, no path through
the immensity of surrendered trees:
the new moon, as if this were a present,
a gift of something observed,
something desired. In the dark

we do our best to dream,
a concoction of holy waters cutting the shoreline
of wake and sleep. No comfort in the window, clouded and black,
the night sky too much even for the lion, even for the owl.
And now to think of endings as well as beginnings,

how does that work? What on the morrow must I leave behind—
gift to the protection of the Stone people, set aside for another time
another life. Twelfth house endings,
a new moon drawn down on sorrows,
and no one likes these tears for long. We are made for cycles

of the come and go of seeds
blown onto a barren landscape of death dreams,
we are made hopeful and like the phoenix and the moon
we come again to dream and believe and wander.
As the dark moon signals abandonment

we can blow on the destiny stone all we like
but when the moon comes to the twelfth house
she mirrors a dark shroud, beckoning, and her ragged face
hides behind the fog of a slow body and a mind on fire.

Violets

We make prayer kintos out of violets
and pass them off between us weeping
the way quiet whispers lose their words
in the thick air of a hedged garden,

We are misled by pale hues
and generous breezes of spring
by too many phrases of birdsong
complicated by a brim of need.
Three pale violet petals held together
with kiss and wish.

We believe,
while the white butterfly says grace
over the iron table, our tea cools
and we let the sun set on our faces.

Mestana

Messy wefts in pale colors:
bleached turquoise faltering in the face of an angry sun
welded to a slash of silver mountain, the rose
of a petal's earliest edge,
the colorless tone of an eyelid at peace. At the edges
death gray, a feathered wing of rightful prayer
darkened by tears. The faintest green washed
again and again, an ocean of aging without grace.
There is no blue, no white. You see why, of course,
here in this linear disorder, they are the colors of warp,
of spirit, of sky, the universal threads that carry us all
untouched by my carelessness.

Villanelle for Gene

A wish, a veil, my lover rising over me,
he knows these wanderings and where they have led—
a midnight moon has pulled me from my bed.

Flushed and disheveled from the dreaming.
Lost in heartbeat's darkness keening
a wish, a veil, my lover rising over me—

What words drift among the covers,
what loss, what gain, what fear has led
this midnight moon has pulled me from my bed.

No comfort in the window clear, no cool air
no simple touch or whisper—
a wish, a veil, my lover rising over me—

I know what I know and I am for the taking,
a hand, a mouth, a breast, sweet sweat,
a midnight moon has pulled me from my bed.

He touches where he may, I have no defense,
returning from my wanderings late and lost.
A wish, a veil, my lover rising over me,
a midnight moon has pulled me from my bed.

Totem Gallery

The Tlingit say that Raven and Eagle share each other's grief,
answering each other's song, and by sharing joy, they also remove each
other's grief.
—museum plaque/Seattle Art Museum

I walked into the quiet and saw a half moon of carved faces,
whale and wolf and bear flanked by two totem poles,
raven and eagle;
and behind, the carved circle the magical opening,
perhaps to the sea or
the unknown that you will now know,
led there by your clan guide.
And in the center you were waiting, upsidedown, red dog,
waiting for my tears, my prayers, waiting for the song to swim
to the surface, and the wet floodrace of what we know
and wish for you—
really, it's the same that we wish for ourselves—
sharing joy, sharing grief, finding our way to the circle,
the center fire, there to listen for the drumming and just be,
just be for a moment raven and eagle,
dog and man, eagle and raven,
man and dog.

My Seed

A drowned mouse in the trough, dull gray and bloated
like the relentless clouds that cast across the ocean
buckle against the cliffs.
It's a hard day to like, even with its number significance, a new year,
one to the forth power means what exactly?
That the countdown starts today,

that each of us is required to choose a kernel of corn, a single seed
in which all new hope will lie?
That we can turn our faces to the sun god
even if he is blanketed by cloud,
and cast our seeds onto the earth,
know what part we play in this puzzle.

One seed, only one.
Restrain the human arc of greed that would take more,
you need only one, tiny, firm button of life affirmation,
your notion of good.
What will it be for you this year?

I'd like to start by hoping for no more drowned mice.
And then add to that no more dead rabbits, deer, bear or birds,
no friend or foe gone.
May your rifles twist, your shot curdle.
May a web of cloud blur your aim,
may your arms weigh heavy, your fingers freeze.

And in that moment,
may you find your conscience delivered before you and bloom,
my seed.

Apology for King Philip's War

The Need:
Tell me how you would settle the score,
a shoreline stranding of tears exists even today—
uncover it and look for the blood and bone.
Tell me what would it take to reconcile a nation's guilt
when you could build a bridge across the great sea lake
on the skulls of the first people,
when their blood could turn the waters dark
and their cries drown the gulls and silence the raven forever.
Explain to me how to apologize
for a war of rage, when my ancestors ravaged the Pequot
as if they were not living beings.

The Call:
Raven, black and fierce
calls me out on a dark moon night,
calls me out for the tallying. He says
Do you think you can escape the curse of generations?
Their guilt runs thick and thicker unless we seek it out,
make it plain.

The Ritual:
Here, do this, he says to me,
Take a scrap of dark red wool,
bead around it finely in white, for tears.
Make a journey to the top of the mountain
and there find a stone, red and thick,
shape that stone into a sharp edge
and with it, scribe a line across your cheek,
and then the other, drawing blood.

Wipe the blood of your ancestor onto the cloth
and fold it sunwise and with ceremony.
Build a fire and come to your knees before the heat,
touch your head to the ground and ask for grace

where there might be none. When the fire is ready
for you, cast the cloth into the fire and turn your back,
turn your back on sixteen generations of wrongdoing,
make it plain. Hold still within the heat of the fire and
make it plain, Raven said.

The Apology:
And so I stand before you to make plain
what you already know,
that your mistake was your kindness. No
thanksgiving here.
There is no apology available great enough.
But those ancestors of mine will have won
if you move forward forgetting Raven and Bear and Snake,
Bird, Frog and Hare,
and if what they whisper to you even now, passes you by
like the beaten wind of an eagle overhead.
Make it plain, make it strong, pull down the spirit
and reclaim what is your right. Build up your fires and dance
on the earth who loves you. Make it plain to all
you have never died.

Unicorn

He's a juvenile, his coat now fully shifted
from the color of hay in sunlight, to soft wet duff.
Young and hungry he steps carefully out of the wood
and comes ahead to the nourished grasses of landscape.
His muzzle is white, as if the gods thought for the briefest
moment to make him albino,
"ah no, they said in unison, a unicorn!"
And so he is, a single sparse branch
undeveloped and raw slicing the middle
of his long countenance,
as if the magic of it might shift our gaze.

What nutrient burr, what glancing blow
what lapse in genetic stream,
what skew made this?
The gait is true, the haunch a perfect target;
hungry, yes, always so in summer here.
Is it time now? Have we done enough?
The condor rises, the deer fall,
and we will step away,
for now we must use the left eye seeing,
warned for the last time.

Prey

I'm standing at the window, sweat blooming
between my breasts, my face hot, brain in disorder,
as still as possible while the moment passes,
breathing, watching, as something solid and dark
pads off into the bushes, my private forest

she goes with the slow gate of the predator
unconcerned, or cautious, a darkness, that's all.
While I'm wondering how it will be when my own time comes,
soon or late, sudden or desperate, doorway or gate,
something solid and dark
pads off into the bushes

and it may be time to follow, to set aside the summer act
and measure progress by the winter gate, full dark broken
by brief and incremental light, my private forest
where paths lead nowhere, and sometimes
something solid and dark pads off into the bushes.

Her notion of survival is the equinox to mine. Haphazard
and gibbous, random deaths. I am over-thinking the moment,
all moments come eventually to this: follow her or not,
this random forest dying, where will we hide then
when something dark and solid
pads off into the bushes?

Peat Fire

Sunday deep in fog,
I build a turf fire, a tell of the landscape
of my belonging. Drinking hot sweet tea—
Gene's grandmother used to say
you could stand a spoon up in it by end of day.

In order to heal you must start at the beginning.
Go back, go back follow the spiral of smoke.

Driving into a somber village, late in the day,
fires are lit, gray on gray the layers of sky
no filter for the senses. It is an ancient memory
this one of fire, peat burning hot in a bed of stone,
cauldron on the boil. The strength of the old oak grove
a lure to us now, our life blood then.

Maybe I struggled on nameless days
peat, dried and cut in random slabs, thrown,
a withy basket strapped to my back. Am I
man or woman, it does not matter, any more
than the day of the week, or the progress of the life.
We do what must be done.
We stay close to the land, and pray for her bounty.
Perhaps, as I often see, my cottage crowns a barren hill,
no visitors come, though the fire stays full and welcoming.
Baskets of herbs, skeins of wool, dark bottles and jars of musty haze,
my spells, my work fill days. Peat fire my perfume.

Driving into a somber village, I don't remember now which one.
I see the tractor idling at the corner,
the young farmer in the phone box.
The mist becomes rain, we are lost in love.
I wonder, where is this place called longing?

Which life calls to you? Which one calls too soon? The ancestors
will be the death of us if we let them through.

I build a turf fire and watch the wood kindling turn to ash,
the turf begin to glow, an ordinary fire, transformed.
It's curious that we have to leave
in order to come back and smell home.
Whether the journey is literal or the musings of a quiet mind,
where will you go?
Where is the mountain of your beginning? Nothing
no thing will come until you begin, begin from there.
I step outside into the fog and touch the iron fence.
Peat smoke fills my senses, this is an ancient memory
shared with blood and bone, ghost and faerie.
Belonging comes, yet still we are alone.

Things to take to Ireland

Tarot fans an invitation before me,
cards in fives, cups of sweet mead, heavy ale provide,
guide, inspire, promise, conceal me.

Gold bangles, perfect circles reveal me,
infinite connection. My mother's
hand detaining me.

Mesa stones, mountains of dreams and dreaming,
smooth worn or jagged peaked
where all this before has brought me.

Dorothy's vase, fragile, bubbled and green,
a totem, an insistence,
what is mine? is me?

Diary words come slowly from me,
painful this departure, material weight,
"we need to get you a smaller journal" she says to me.

Gene, of course, comes with me,
lover who knows me
provides, and which other friends will last?

That green quilt I love,
how curiously easy precious objects
fade before me.

Howard's violin—for in Ireland
there is always time
and time again for learning.
the glass bear a child's treasure
where this obsession began,
now elevated to totem.

Poetry, mine and theirs,
Oliver, a recluse to mimic,
Yeats, Emily, who else is there?

snake ring, boldly on my right hand,
third eye on my left,
family of the universe connect me.

cats and dogs can't stay behind me,
they are the watchers, the comfort of friends,
they are the guideposts, Sirius, oracles of stars.

Hawk Medicine

He landed on the dead pine
and seemed to step back, against the trunk,
and disappeared. In the fog, I wasn't sure—
had I seen him at all? Then he turned his head,
a brief, quick shift, and yes, he was there,
looking like the tree trunk,
invisible in the crepuscular fog,
shadows made by the wet western edges of the forest,
white and muzzy stillness. He blinked perhaps,
and so did I. He's hunting as the dark comes on,
invisible, stealthy, fearless.

We don't know that word: fearless.
We have many worries, cataloged and worn from airing.
Some of them have graduated to the status of fear.
And so if we could take hawk medicine, a spoonful at a time,
at dusk, we would salve the weeping wound of fear,
heal it with a small but consistent dose of courage.
What we need is to be invisible, in power, watching for the
small things that will feed a life and make it grow fearless.
Be patient, practice stillness. Fold our wings close and lean—
lean back against the mother—become One, Hawk.

For whatever reason, known only to him,
it is time to move on. No hurry, wings open,
and he is gone. Life is that simple. Live in fear,
be the prey, or be fearless. It takes nothing special,
just step back against the tree,
and disappear.

Crooked Path, Crooked Path

Red Moon rising, the blood mother bonding
what is your crooked path, crooked path?
Here in the sun, unseen moon shedding,
the air crackles and warnings throb in my breast.

Crooked path, crooked path, random
actions of simple hunger,
like the small birds in the new mown grass,
this is a feast for an unknown future.

Red moon, red moon, fill me
even if it is bad news, it is something—
when death is the gravitation of the soul
along a crooked path

crooked path, diverted, distorted,
disillusioned and yet, devoted. Storming
out a place, a plot that is my own, one
destination, one determination, crooked path

crooked path.

Wedding Dress

Boxing Day was her day,
her dress a tulip of champagne satin
as much sex as 1944 would allow,
she must have felt like a million bucks as they'd say.
Every curve on display, an arched dark eyebrow,
she might have thought it was ridiculous
but still I'll bet she loved it, all eyes her way,
everyone gathered, united and silent
for once.
Many years ago I tried on her dress,
it's in the same box as my own. Nothing
about it fit,
a smudge of Elizabeth Arden pink on the edge
telling tales of what came next.
Funny how one day changes a life.

The Justice Birds

Everywhere I look there are dead birds—
A gray jay trapped in the summer house, eviscerated
by the old cat, shore birds turning on an oily scree, shock and death,
and yet no one talks about them, no one speaks of the indecency of
spilling our casual mortality across species, no one is counting,
no one admitting the crime is so much greater than the easy loss.

The ravens call a concordance and discuss what they see,
what would they do if they could see that far,
what wrath would they bring, what judgment would fall,
like the feathers of the gray jay, blown across a simple carpet—
no eyes, no heart, only the long tail of gut and spare open body,
betrayed,

and betrayer. The call is to a reckoning. A reduction.
Who stays and who must go?
Who works entwined in the pattern of the universe,
who jabs and pierces and bucks against the tides? The stench
increases, the weight presses most on those who cannot defend.
We watch, we cry, some of us pretend, we scoop and shovel
never-ending piles of raped sand, fathoms of blue turned brown
and overhead, each day, fewer birds cry.

We are so capable of horror, so inured to the crimes,
we think only human loss important,
we are bleeding the earth dry,
our greed has pushed the threshold of death's mirror,
you think this isn't worse?
You don't know what happens when the earth
bleeds dry. Every other living creature knows how to live in balance,
we have not learned, we will not learn.
Now, the ravens will decide.

Charlemagne Standard

It's not just the slick hyper white paper, the narrow pinch
a treasure map line, a thumb's portion,
it's also the quick slice of ligatures, the brazen y dangling
taking more than her share of the space.

I love
the elegance of an E with swirling curls, so much excess
for a simple muted vowel. And the Queen of letters, the Q
when she's allowed to stand alone
without you
just an apostrophe to trail her brocaded train.

I love the book as much as its matter.
Sometimes I'll pull Everyman off the shelf
just to relish her India papers,
or pull the cap off my Waterman
and place a tiny star on an acid free field of snow
beside a perfect line
of type.

The Clue

It would be good if the days took on more meaning,
instead they slide inexorably one into the other
defined by small chores and the kinds of aches and pains
one can count on. Too many blank pages

and suddenly this notion of journal keeping seems perhaps
moot. Even a record of the weather won't serve any future reader,
not with the cataclysm we are insisting on, the one that kissed
predictability on the lips

and shoved her on her way. Yes, oh yes,
we will revolve, evolve, rotate, and mandate
and make ourselves big and ferocious,
leave playing dead to other creatures

the ones with hairless tails,
they will inherit the earth once we've done;
and with this lethargy of late years, a retiring body—
no I'm not made of stone—

but a thousand or so years from now
that footprint I just made in the mud
behind the garage, that,
that will matter to someone.

Sing to God

There are no footprints through the snow, no trail
connecting some narrow cart track to the heavy wooden door.
No god lives here now, no people huddle in the center circle of his
    light—
wishing they were warm, wishing they were heavy with great heaps
    of hot food,
wishing they had been spared Stalin, avoided Lenin's gaze, wishing
god had let them be instead of sending them the trial that is this
    cold,
this perilous country.

If I were Russian, I would bundle into my fox fur hat and thick dark
    coat,
lapels obscuring my mouth and nose, saddle the lone black horse
to the sleigh and sail off toward the specter that is god in this church
    of loneliness,
the waxed runners singing in the slick ice and snow,
and in my head even before the great old door opens
I will hear the voices of men too cold to be in love, the chorus
trailing across the snowy world like smoke from a fire going out,

and then, inside, robust and full throated in their drunken song,
they sing to god, sing to god.

Poem a Day Sonnet

Think how productive we would be—
couldn't be as daunting as it seems
the paper alone we would count in reams—
a poem a day, hey, maybe three.

Write about food and cooking and sex
make believe, god —just your best
just words, that's all, and then rest.
maybe a spell or two or a hex, then

Lay your head on the pillow of your words.
Nap knowing you've done all your chores
quick before baby or hubby or those bores
who mark time by the sucklings and the wars

Come calling, come knocking on your door.
For the poem is why you live,
within it contained all you can give,
stanza and line, one two three four.

They needn't be special or erudite
They don't need to be long,
or good or even a song

They needn't give you a fright
or goosebumps or even
master some outlandish believin'.

Clutter

This is a cumulative effect,
at first a sly sleight of hand, just ignore this or that—
set these papers, a few unopened envelopes,
an upside-down list of things to do—set them here,
and then casually cover them with newly folded towels.
Out of sight, these random projects find mooring
deep in the seat of my honest worker Yankee ancestry,
and like an old elm they put out roots and begin to buckle
my surface life, until one Sunday I see that I have grown
idle, bound in stasis, and nothing new will happen here
until I sweep clear the mundane web, open the new page,
uncap my pen, and begin again.

The Death Horses (Italian sonnet)

When death comes down and takes us for a ride,
old hauntings pierce the early hours with tears
when unbidden springs the catalog of my fears
then mortality is master of time and tide

and though the distant ocean rushes through,
and though the rain is soft and whispers care,
memory drags me toward the deathly mare
snorting, pounding, jangling and true.

To live in youthful forgetfulness
to shun the wisdom of collected woe
spurs and spirits remain all that I know.

Fear stands pillion waiting to possess
to engulf my heart with melancholy so well
it seems all present time must sound its knell.

Blue Heron

When I was small
the Blue Heron was a pub,
a fisherman's bar really, a landmark
that told us our day long journey by car
was nearly over.

The air in the shiny new Packard had blown our eyes dry,
once we got past the Chippewa flowage—I loved that name—
we looked for wigwams and wooden Indians
and only saw broken down trailers and
plastic swimming pools covered in weeds,

and we stared out the window, always asking
'how much farther' over and over again,
and the keener geographer of us saw the signs
and each bend looked different to him
and then, there was the billboard, "Blue Heron

beer and bait, lodging and moorage"
the faded prehistoric bird a colossus,
an anchor. We were nearly there.
Nearly free, our imaginations had stored up
a winter's worth of story, of smell,

warm sand, damp smoky clothes, children's games—
we never got tired of the play or the acting.
We left our hearts there, planted by the old tree
safe in the soft dell grown over with fernleaf and moss,
another year gone, another tether lost.

Shoes

I had a pair of shoes
20s style, pale beige leather heels.
I never wore them,

along with the cloche hat
and the boiled wool coat
they were a future

I was waiting to become:
full enough, expanded and free—
maybe loved

waiting for an evening,
a ride of desire
an opportunity to grow.

I had a pair of shoes,
worn with silk stockings,
clipped and gartered,

bare flesh in a small space
a glimpse of desire...
I never wore them.

Under G

Four white plumed ducks settled gentle as paper boats,
one solitary grebe, unmatched and longing. I'd like *grebe*
to be a verb, one could say 'having no partner grebed her deeply.'
or *her mannerisms felt grebious to those who sat at table with her.*
Brown, dull, and foolish in love, intense and servile in loneliness,
we grebe when we swim alone in dark shallow waters, rudderless
without a clear footing or intent. Grebe.
And then just up on the page lies *glebe.*
We see it often in small English villages,
Glebe House, like The Moorings or Rose Cottage,
there's one in every valley,
every crevice of countryside.
Glebe, a churchman's living, archaic, but also
simpler than that, a field, a piece of land.
No one every says *I'm going to mow the glebe now,* but they could.
Glebe implies a relationship between man and his land,
ownership, patronage, the right to pull something from the earth.
Verbed, glebe becomes the act of wresting profit from the fields
by godly right—humans are the only species that do that. Glebe.

Winter Night

There must be something we should have done today,
some way to encourage the sense of honoring brought by candle
   flame,
by smoldering oak logs, the scent of nutmeg and apples. Something
might allow us to maintain this sense of our selves as one,
connected here and cast across time to ancestors:
ancient ones long missed.

We sigh and breathe their names in whispers
and the words make candles flicker—
ghostly memories of moments long past—
those times we were unaware, careless, all knowing.
We've had the chance to say what needed saying
even to ghosts, they listen everywhere.

There must be something we should have done today,
but companionable silence is a grace we need to know,
like comfort food, loyal dogs, and silent snowfall
love is as deep as an eave in drift piled high with logs
yet to burn. Make the fire soft enough to touch,
that's my advice, make it burn long and steady.

Now words are occasional devices
we use to conjure and cast. There is more
to be found in the flames, or better yet
in the startling skyfull of imaginings,
a Moon now who leads us across
sighing before the Milky Way sea.

Monk's Mind

I'm drawn to the devout life,
the kind the Buddhist boys in orange have -
some remote hill top refuge deep in jungle -
no that won't do, how about
a craggy orthodox pile in Greece?
but not that one near Athens, too near
the beer and ouzo,
or, here's an idea, a chilly French
slab of marble somewhere in the forest of Brittany
someplace where genius will arrive
without promises and imbrications of intention-
where each thought might be a direct connection
to Other, where I could take up the rosary
and tell the stories of every one of the gods,
line them up in glory. I could make bread there.

But first I need to answer a few questions,
I'm plagued by how we managed to short change the tip
to that waiter in DC,
and should we have tipped the strong armed woman
whisking batter for crepes on Mont Saint Michel?
I've worried, did I never hear from that charming person
I met long ago, it seemed we had so much to say,
was there a tragedy involved or just my bad graces?
I need to know why dandelions close up at night,
why lying is everyone's first impulse, why
even when there is a ring around the moon
still it does not rain.
I'm concerned I should have made excuses,
explained about the mismade bed, never left the dog
home alone, told someone at the airport that I had no
money, no words.
I should have lined up with the rest of them,
paid the piper his due, then there might be
a place to go to— the shore of some remote lake—
and walk there by the clear water's edge.

Sleep

I've been trying to replace thirty years of inadequate sleep,
or at least this is what I tell myself, as yet again
I head for bed in the middle of the afternoon;
the promise of the cool touch of cotton, the filtered ocean
rush of air, and even though the birds won't quiet down, still
their tedious sense of joy so persistent at dawn has given way.
Now they are on watch and watch, piping up for the occasional
  predator.
I'm desperate for sleep that lasts beyond the single hour—
I could function as the bell-toller's watch, breaking out into a sweat
with the regularity of blooded moons and mystery tides.
No matter that all the literature says we can't make up for the loss.
  We chase
an illusion, sleeping with angels, upstairs on a real bed, a bed
we come back to later for sustenance, for life. But sleeping,
sleeping the way a lily pad walks the waves of the lakeshore,
sleeping the way old cats and tiny babies sleep the sleep of spirits
at rest, all forgiven. This is the timelessness I long for, a restorative
tea of no thinking, cloudy leaves sugared with soft creamy down.
I'd let myself fall deeply, I would, and pull a great vision out of some
  darkness;
something later I could write about without tripping, without stones
or silence. I think that eight or ten hours of purgatory each night
must produce some whey, some juicy liquid poured from a caring
  Muse.
And if the deepest sleep comes not in the dark, but with the
  brightness of the day,
then all right, I'll come up again, up to bed and give myself up,
cast spells of spent nights, and form a prediction for one more
  tomorrow.

The Lilac

All I have are intentions.
A mass of green perfect leaves brush the clapboards,
each one an idea, a collection of sibilant words,
and now and then, early in the season, one lone
small effort at blooming. The lilac

blooms outside the smallest window of the house,
an exhausted tentative effort at fragrance,
the palest color, barely qualified as lilac.
And yet, the stems and branches are upright,
sturdy and taller than I, up against a wall
in a wind of change.

What I want is the overpowering cloy of scent
a Midwestern childhood remembrance
back when the wet struggle of each breath filled
with newly mown grass and opulent pendulous blooms:
the lilacs and peonies of memory, when we could
sit all day in the garden, and watch the giant ants propagate
as the condensation on our lemonade fell unheeded to our knees.

The Witching Stick

By the door a pole of iron topped with a cat head bell,
this is no talking stick, no story pole,
this is the remnant of Zoroaster's wrath:
a cold evil guard, malevolent fung shui.
We can see how Fire became God,
the magic of the Forge, the alchemical giant Iron.
We can see how the smith became holy,
his fire the Fire of Power. Ugly lumps of earthly char
becomes an iron pipe, a weapon, god's warrior
wealding this cat face. Not so sinister, Zoroaster's cat,
but imagine him raised in an angry mob
bloodied young men, chanting wrath of god evil
the witching stick striking upward to the sky,
bells tinkling.

Nail Polish

Paint your toenails blue
in lieu of a tattoo that will only wrinkle
and pock with age, no doubt a serpent
or lizard it would just slip gradually down
your arm and land puffing around a swollen
spotted wrist,
you'd have to stare at it every day, poking
here and there, stretching the finely lined skin
to see the adder's tongue, the rattle tail now
more like a Christmas ornament,
and every time you raised a glass
there it would be, a reminder of the time
you forgot yourself and took a dare,
pretended some extroversion you knew
wasn't there, no
no pink hair, no bells around the ankles
no bright red sports car, no dancing in the streets,
no tattoo.
Paint your toenails a temporary blue,
secure in the knowledge that no one looks
down at you, and the magic that remains
is simply air, a gentle cushioning of a skeleton
crumbling, the invisible pillow of death on the run.

Forest Fire

The sky, a miserable mirror,
predicts the horseman's visit in June.
The sun wakes up the west wind
ruffling new born ducks
beneath the cloudy pool in the garden.
Darker now, in charred remains
this earth will ever be—
after the park lifts its ban, and mud and rain
return when summer ends.

The Fear Box

Fear lives in that little box with the wiggly hinge.
It's a sorcerer able to giant its shadow:
one minute quiet, at bay,
the next the monster under the bed.
I would like to learn the banishing words,
the spell for fearlessness, the one
that would make me unblinking,
unbound. I know no antidote to worry,
even love, smotherer of so many emotions,
can't arm itself against Fear.
There is nothing to confront,
that box is within, open.

Open a little, or a lot, lid mawing,
a cavern of dare. Let go, it says, control
may be worse than fear, turn your back,
it says, see whose hand touches your neck.
Open a little, nay, open all the way,
cast an origami rain fall of these little fears,
mites of darkness not yet brutal formed.
Open your whole self to the universe,
purge every little thing and be new,
be ready, be the virgin to the lover bold.
Close the box. Turn away.
It's only one day. One new day.

Sphinx

It's what we all want:
to be inscrutable, solid,
and yet, instead, our tribes are eroded
frayed,
a composite of flayed intentions.
There is no purpose to assembly;
we are not connected for that.
Instead, we send moths to the flame,
we have a surplus—
disaffected, disconnected, disoriented men,
armed with their gods.
Who can argue with that?

From the right vantage point
the sphinx looks like the head of a penis—
the tour guide gleefully pointed this out to us;
is this where we are? Are there so many
of us
that we must destroy each other
before we dialog about truth? Is
it really a matter of last man standing
when that man is so reduced in possibility?

And in all this, where are the invisible women?
The women who breed for these men,
who cook, and bear their children,
who want perhaps even more than they
in the end, it is the women who must go
go to the sphinx, lie down and spread their legs again;
because all of the men in their singular tribe
of blame and hatred not once,

not once, have they thought
of their women.

Paris

What is the sound of longing?
Is it courtyard church bells calling to matins?
Is it the soft glow and bitter smoke of candles lit?
Is the soft swish of robes, the clear high notes of mass sung
by angels?

Is it the smell of morning baked bread, the luxury of coffee,
the turning of pages, devouring a place, a time, a sense of belonging,
a longing for immersion.
Is it the cold and uneven tiles of the cathedral floor,
the reminder of awe and of our small part.

Is it the river flow, the cobbled streets, the garden walls
geraniums pocketed here and there?
Can a longing like this be soothed? Be fed? Be tempered?
Can longing become belonging, for so it seems a lifetime
then and now.

Where shall we tuck this longing? What small space
have we made in our hearts for place? Foundation, essence,
promise, tucked and covered gently with our hands
in prayer.

Haikus for France

We sip pale sweet tea
slowing our minds with small sighs—
praise for the spring sun.

New grass, a warm sun
we're reckless in our welcome,
the cows push ahead.

Bright green bistro chairs
two glasses half drunk, sun sets
we reach for a shawl.

Arm in arm with you
once high upon the mountain
everyone was god.

Haiku, little words
like confetti from the sky—
joy in tiny slips.

Hortus Botanicus

Hope and Promise are the funny twin sisters of spring.
They live down a lane past houses we wouldn't set foot in,
and I don't know what they do the rest of the year,
their petticoats dripping with fog, their floppy flower hats
covered with the dust of last fall,
but in the spring they are two jewels, strutting virgins, they dance
down the nursery aisles laughing, calling us to follow, and to dream.

Hope's real name is Wisteria, (her mother had a sense of humor);
she requires all of our admiration,
and a good propping up now and then.
Promise holds back, checks your finger nails for dirt
—green dirt is best—
she wants to know what's in it for her,
what makes this spring the time,
and where do you live anyway? What's your zone?

What we want is to follow Hope and Promise around the rows
tight packed with containers of just flowering futures,
we want to pick the very thing, take it home, and drink tea
while we ponder placement and predators.
Hope and Promise sit lightly with us,
bright and shy as though their guardian, some maiden aunt,
stands nearby with bits of logic, summer sun,
and a gopher or two in her pocket.

For now, just now, while the fairies roam the rootlands
spreading encouragement,
we want nothing to do with accountability,
that's for another day.

Orca

Before we seek higher ground,
we should walk the littoral zone.
Turn and watch the footprints
wash and fill, you're here, you are gone.
Before we stake a claim,
wonder what right we have,
as the sand sloughs the shoreline clean,
brushes over our toes, tugging, sinking.
Before we move on looking for forests to clear,
mountains to bore, fields to barren, stand
in the space between water and earth
and wonder at your birth, your death, and
all that will come and go with tides and time—
flencing until your skeleton shines,
beneath a bright mooned sky.

Home Alone

This is a sample
an early morning without you.
This is what it might be like, after, long
after the scatter and tensions of occupation disperse.
After each room releases its own measure of sorrows
some emptiness would descend.
Slowly, then, I would reimagine, reoccupy
the spaces left by you.

The dog would still guard your chair
—that's a given—
(there is no logic in love)

But I would learn not to fight the dawn: perhaps
I'd start drinking your coffee
sit in the old rocker on the porch, finally
make a pact with the sun.
Listen to the thrush
and wonder about cycles,
straining for what might come
of the deafening silence.

Car Ride

My suitcase, empty, sits between floors
a turning point, the coffin corner of a life,
not, somehow, put away—
away with the ancestors and their diary clothes—
just empty.

Sitting backwards in the seat,
looking out the Packard's window:
what we have left behind— the summer joy—
scattered along the single lane leafy road.
There is nothing in front of us now.

The robin's egg blue wool of the car's seat
rubs my sunburned thighs, a way to feel,
marking a tiny moment — one that might be
the best, or the last. Watching the road leave
no one can tell.

The photographs, worn and pale keepsakes
bring on that childhood flood:
there was happiness, yes, but there
was also the absence of longing, a pure
complete moment, neither forward

nor back. Now, growing and knowing,
a long sequential calendar of forwards and
backwards, of longing, as if propelled by that one
single car ride, now as then no control, still
looking backwards out the window on the past.

Easter Rising

Late April brings a cold wind to the north.
That late Sunday, we drive through barren villages
shuttered and dry, no Guinness today, no joy.
Instead, we pass cars full of men in dark wool jackets
pale fierce faces set to the windows.
They carry a rage like coals of an old burn,
as an echo of drums calls them out.

The women have been to church,
but now they huddle indoors, no washing
on the line, no babies in carriages on the walks.
Violence visits, a hush descends,
an echo of drums calls them out.

Men in cars, racing out of the villages
collecting like ants to a dead hand
both sides exactly the same until
banded together on each side of a pale line,
Orange and Green with hearts on fire
an echo of drums calls them out.

We pass them heading north to Belfast
our little rental car stark and obvious,
we carry no fierceness, we shiver at their rage.
By the map we divert our course, circle away
from men with clubs and drums, looking for the soft
woman that is Ireland, heading south to a republic
as echoes of drums call them out.

Every year they do this, mark the Rising day,
losers and winners, both sides
kindle the fire for another generation, bring
the boys out, bring them out, they carry a rage
like coals of an old burn
as echoes of drums call them out.

Zhivago Sky

The blues and grays of winter light
trees bare of leaves now dark wraiths
where I can imagine flight:
the witch moving swift, rustling
all sharp edges and frozen surface,
lines of merging wilderness,
lake well frozen beneath pure white.
Zhivago Sky is a ball of yarn—
more shades than one can name
and yet so few are the winter colors, ones
of a season I thought I had forgotten.

To walk deep in snow powder,
to crackle on hard snow surfaces,
unsure, booted, tentative
wrapped double deep in cloaks of wool
all blue and gray and pale:
the only living thing,
to knit up the care of winter light
in a long streaming shawl of
Zhivago Sky blue, to wrap wide,
and fight the beautiful melancholy of winter
as it closes quietly around.

The Selkie Wife

where have I left it, and left it too late?
It is over me like a skin
slick, supple and shining.
Light all the candles, winter has come.

Inertia & Momentum

Inertia and Momentum, two
girls who met on a Beirut street corner
sometime back in 1960, where—
along with the tides of moons, the call to the mosque,
the *wine dark* Mediterranean lure,
the repeating courses of pain and blood—
suddenly found an awareness of requirement—
of things one could not avoid—
a forward motion unstoppable,
accompanied by the cloudy sense of stasis.
A long tangled elastic web of unknowing
hard as a man's seeking hands. Inertia:
she's a veil of wind and air, a breeze
blown of insignificance, immune
to Momentum, this physics insidious,
like a stranger's gaze, disappointment like
the final reach of a precipice
the deep cliffs of the neverending.
To hesitate, to wait,
to move or to go: whatever
we desire, some things are inevitable.

On the Wind

Comes the sea, now fresh and soft
now menacing and fierce
comes the sounds of ducks if you listen well
talking of romance
and what to have for tea,
come the hectoring trucks
jake breaking down the grade.
If the ducks don't mind,
why should I?
Come the swans, heading south,
how beautiful to be pure white.

Comes my love on the wind,
calling me home.

Solitary Loon

A single molting bird,
so far no partner, no drop in temperature
no deep blood reminder makes him go.
He doesn't consider the journey—
perhaps he lost his mate over summer—
what predatory sling caught this perfect life
and tore it apart, leaving solitude
wanted or not?
What motivation remains?
Partners gone,
we might all bob along in the middle—
lake-bound, sorrowful,
until we have waited too long
mourned too well,
until Death reaches out
a solution, a forgiving. A loon
always mournful, calling,
calling, raiment of old feathers
like my best old rags
a comfort in the shedding:
then sorrow is a naked bird
a solitary loon distant on the lake.

Oh Rain

Oh Rain! kiss me everywhere—
there is not a moment to lose.

Mare's Tails

I was wondering why the well went dry—
and stepping back looked up
to see those elusive coltish clouds
moving east—so far beyond the tops of trees
they took me back to a different place
where campfire burned and water lapped
and Earth swayed her fernleaf skirts.

Daguerreotype: Emily Dickinson

We always remember them in sepia,
pallid browns and sad silks,
we can feel the pinch of boots
nailed with tiny rusting hinges
the way Emily was nailed to her room:
her viewshed a funeral perimeter,
perpetual bad moon on the rise.
She might have closed the door
and hovering behind a lace curtain
fingered leaves of thick yellowing paper
a scrounger's bounty, scavenger's hoard,
small drops of brilliant indigo ink
her rare delight. She'd wet her finger
and smear the words,
smiling for the camera.

Mountain Lions

Two lions on a winding path,
in my dreaming we meet
but I know they are my fear:
a surfacing of insecurity
I sleep, but somehow my real self
has gone out the window
down the path
looking for lions.

Of course,
they are there, out there
in the woods, vigilant,
perhaps bedded under the cracked
gnarled old pines away from the house,
away from my window.
Or they are standing right below—
how would I know?

It's a dark moon night
a waxing of senses and emotion
ahead of a fall eclipse, a testing
of nerve,
shall we be afraid of the lion
or secure in the knowing of her yellow eyes?
Who can we protect if we sleep
the sleep of deep dreaming?

Lions padding back and forth,
I know them,
like me they are hungry with
an impulse for survival
that makes me wake every morning
when I could so easily drift away,
that dreaming is like their breathing—
and now and then I hear them yawn and growl.

Leave-Taking

There is the unexpected kind,
an unbidden telephone rings,
an unacceptable face appears at the door.
There is the tragic kind, the loss too soon,
a life not played out.

There is the deliberate goodbye,
a means to an end. There are lesser tragedies:
friends who need going, methods of quartering
our days which no longer serve, no longer
bring us to the 24th hour in a single piece.

There is a sense of life passing, of days of birth
numbered, counted and counting down.
Always the question: what is your legacy?
What should it have been?
And could you truly have altered course?

Departures imply an imperative arrival—
like polishing the silver, or
rearranging the furniture, something
cleansed is expected, we are caught in a dualism
in which choice is the main ingredient.

It is when we have not chosen
that the departed are mourned. No
accidents, no freaks of nature's terrible
force, nothing to face, nothing to fear,
a simple leave-taking, no goodbyes.

In many ways we never stop,
never end the shifting of alliances,
always we are searching for the equity
of a calm spirit in a safe body
in the sweet motion of a life

well loved.

Sticks and Stones

Compromise might just be the evil twin,
the weakness of a grafted heart
a misery of the theoretical forest
a deciduous darkness — no paths taken—
we would have regrets unspoken
marked events where false steps won
where love was simply not enough.
This is where we cannot meet—
no center line, just those zig zags
promising a stop. Compromise
is no angel of mercy, no zen hesitation.

There are some things we simply must have.
Without them the withering begins.

Call Me By My Name

These alliances we have made, the good ones,
find their place at the table, chairs side by side.
You call me by my name when we talk
and that alone makes my words count for more,
as if you have my heart and soul in your generous hands
and are pointing here and there
the things I could make better for myself,
for us, for you.

You call me by my name—
no one else does that,
as if I exist after all, beyond
just an accumulation of intent, regret,
the distance of inattention.
You say this or that and I open my ears, my eyes,
and take in some direct connection
the one beyond the words, beyond the commonplace:
talking of dogs, and friends, and places we've been.

You call me by my name
and suddenly we're talking with the gods
holding time at bay
bringing something safe and precious between us:
the magic of the moment.

Persephone's Nails

Persephone and her nail pairings—
only the Greeks would make much of bathroom floor detritus,
well, perhaps the Romans too.
That my nail pairings should drop like precious fruit
or form the core constituent of a cauldron of frothed and bitter elixir
is enough to make a crone laugh.
Cackle: that's what useful nail pairings should be called.

What I notice is that nails are a measurement of activity.
Cut short and fine like a school boy's, my hands become strong,
interesting— they are like no one else's hands— capable
of a fine pen stroke; cut fine, new stalks,
my fingers, dented and freckled and banded in captive gold,
invisible promises lie beneath the tips, what it is to be woman
of the gods.

Dog and Raven

The mating pair live in the wood,
not far, they want to keep an eye out,
keep an intimate connection with our doings...
Nested tall in the old pine, a dark smudge in shadows.

Every morning they assemble:
before we've unlocked the doors,
before we've opened the curtained rooms
before the dogs come out to play

they dry off the nighttime glaze of dew
and fly small circles testing wingstrength
chatting about their plans for the day
an alarm for the dawn.

Midmorning they are at their chores
patching nests, hunting, yodeling through their lovesong.
And then it's time to play.
The raven has learned to bark,

he barks, and the dog runs to the base of the tree
and barks back. He swoops from tree to tree
and then takes off, a low level aerial dive
and cast around the house

dog in pursuit, 'round they go.
Now and then the raven stops
and they have a chat. Had enough? he says.
Dog barks.

Early evening, dogs at their supper
safe inside, Raven wants to play,
he swings a slow easy curve around the house
window level - are you in there, dog? Come out.

There is comfort to their routine,
an agreement between species,
a level playing field between earth and air
predator to predator, herder, trinket player, friends.

Sonnet - On Aging

Now is the folding time
even against the powerful waves of blossomed spring
we close the shutters and turn to sorting things
in that mind room where now we are blind.

Grasping breaths from a caged line,
we waited too long to learn to sing.
We wait for something no one will bring,
in invisible cages gilt, wrought and fine.

We swear we will not age,
not separate from life
not without our mark made firm,

but days wander across the page
of our knowing and known strife
and it's true, even old, we did not learn.

Little Pieces

Mostly, I live in some ill-defined future
a scene, a setting
to which I am constantly adding ornament:
a catalog of compensations.
And though they are not born of regret
these little pieces of perceived goodness
are like broken stars aflame.
They give me moments of unsettling, tentative hope,
layering the means by which today
becomes something useful,
some collection of masking valance
that renders the obscenities of decay moot
leaving only beauty behind.

Mapping

The landscape of a foggy Saturday morning
after coffee and the refinement of deliberate food,
not the after thought it usually is,
define an edge to this thing fear,
map perimeters that lie surface deep
between the left hand and the heart.
This is a delicate walk stretching out time
in an uncomfortable dance,
the practicality and logic of a knitted comfort
variegated occupation of a mind
that might lie elsewhere a moment too long and
invite the mapping of fear as anticipation:
the dread we know when waking
on a clear day is not joy.
Mapping the edges of the unknown, a fool
and his string theory left
where exhilaration is a loop turned upon itself.

Alchemy (for Gene)

I'm looking for a visceral response:
I want you hard
your lips parted
your hands flexing.

When I write for you
I want words to come flowing back
from every part of your body,
so that I can pluck them from
the soft places of you,

a conjurer, forming lines together
like the flapping of sparrow's wings,
light and free. When my words
for you chain themselves together,
knit in so many unexplainable rows,

when they and you as mark are one,
then, Beloved, just then, the magic comes.

Rhumb Line

If I drew the heartline
between you and me
it would take more
than Hannibal and his elephants
to chart the line:
a latitudinal rhumb line tether
knotted with magical numbers
signal only to ourselves

tugging always
no way to float free
a great air balloon
of contained significance,
each other a line
latitude to the sky
where your star and mine
shine side by side.

untitled

Withdraw.
The heart can only hold
so much.

Little Light Shining

Little light shining,
Little light will guide them to me.
My face is all lit up,
My face is all lit up.
—   Kate Bush, *And Dream of Sheep*

I want to know if you love him to distraction,
that the want of him is a winged beast
who has plucked and pecked a great hole between your breasts.
I want to see that you have peeled your skin clean of the pale bones
that hold you barely standing,
searching for the truth of his touch, The Fool at the edge of reason.
I want to hear the silent piercing cry that wells in your eyes each
    morning
as you realize once again you have not escaped the Dreadful and his
    Shadowchild.

Or is it light you are despairing? Reaching for what is hidden in fog,
a moonbeam path across open water.
Is it spacious dreaming that eludes you, imprisons you in this
    wanting,
the bedcovers a wet mass tumble of tears?
When flying is what is called for, why is the melancholy of fog your
    mother?
How is it that this gray stillness caresses and restrains you?

I want to know if your love is desperate,
or in your grief have you covered the mirrors in shrouds of crepe
and stopped the old clock ticking?
Have you dismembered your self and set it out, a fragile stem
ready to bolt. Did you
do that for him?
A little light shining, one refracted shaft of what? What do you seek,
the taste and touch and smell of him or
the promise that exists because he existed?

Take down your hair. Go down the fragile stairs,
 kneel on the stones of the shoreline.
Sweep your naked arms, fingers splayed,
cast your self across the shadow of the moonlit seabed.
Who do you see?

Chaos Comes

Chaos comes in small quick packages,
brightly lit or brassy loud,
a reminder,
an eclipse with your name on it,
evil come home.

While there is no avoiding the moment,
the message, a clear and blinding
darkness scatters the words of comfort,
drags the witch of misfortune from her bed.
Chaos comes.

We strive for order, we long
for the symmetry of a spiraled shell
for the cycle of birth and death
to meet us more than half-way:
neither too soon, nor too late.

When Chaos comes
we have stepped out of sync
away from the unconscious rhythm
that sets our personal parade
our star in the constellation.

Often, we know it's coming
we sent an invitation, personally scribed:
come, witch, come
I've reached my limit.
Can Chaos bail me out?

Chaos is the black dog of despair,
the black cat of misstep and distrust
the black wind of fortune lost
the black sky deep in a new moon night
A black Damascene sword turned into a final few words.

Come, witch, come
a shrieking is what we need now
a universal smack of reason,
Chaos has come quick
too quick to turn around.

The Sunday Oracle

I come from the place of the Black Sisters
and I bring news of war and extinction.
Name a religion that denies this as their right?
Virgil wrote these lines two thousand years ago,
when the water was clean, and the plumbing worked,
and beautiful art filled the walls and courtyards of
a civilized empire. How far have we come?
How close to the Stygian reality do we hover? Gleeful
at the notion of brother killing brother.

I come from the place of the Black Sisters
and I bring news of war and extinction.
Can you tear yourself away
from the marketplace
of politics?
From the mongering of fear, ritual sacrifices on
the broad highway of monotony?
When will there be enough blood for you?

I come,
I come from the place of the Black Sisters
and I bring news of war and extinction.
Weep and regret, for you are too many words
away from luminous. Now you can only gawk
empty-handed, there are no prayers for this,
no poses that ring true, no manual, maker
or lord to bring you through.
Wait and prepare, for the last one
the last one to come and go.

I come,
and I bring news of your extinction,
a roiling dust ball of death all around,
death of the mind,

the reduction of brain to
the reading room of the blind. Listen, now,
listen,
I come from the place of the Black Sisters
and I bring news.

Through a window brightly lit

Through a window brightly lit
a darkness engages
moth and wing—
the fox is quiet in his den.

Home

What touch holds you here?
Where is home?
that deep soul sense of belonging,
the absence of fear
and you, my friend.

Clootie Ties

It is a vicious game of tag,
as if, like in school, we line up
and count off our luck by the odds.
We all come away aching, shaken,
thirsty for the water of clarity
seeking the clean prayer cloth,
the cool deep well.

What binds us beyond this fear
is a burden and a gift. Some
woman-tide measurement, it is
nothing and it is everything, unknowable
yet still we understand— the way
our grandmothers found it,
blood thread, blooming.

Cover your head with rags
gleaned from grandmother's scarves,
close your eyes and wonder
how we came to this day, what
blessings have depended
on the accident of life, a game
of chance sorted and cast wide.

Place your fears on the tree of life:
hawthorn, apple or oak, in whispers
come fine and long. Tear
a scrap of linen, mark it well,
give it to the wind to bear
give it to the sun, the moon,
the silver rings of ancient tunes.

Fly the flag of woman song
find the one place, the only place
where you survive. Fly the ties
that bind earth and sky, mark
a measure of all that will be.
There is no doubt that now,
surely now, we can fly.

Seven Sisters

That rose bush is invasive, he says,
like the hand of god, one day. It's true
ropey thorns would like to push between
chipped lines of green painted hinge;
join her in the kitchen for dark tea
and disjointed conversations with the old ones.
Rattling china, Herself (she's dead now and so
we will speak of her less and less),
and faded words will be read out.

But he cut it quick
knowing full well no one ever cuts a climber.
And now the old windowglass shows her age,
distorts the beseeching distant coastal pines.
They are like a wiccan grove of bent old crones
blowing east, desperate for calm and sunrise.

She has taken a lover in the old way.
And when she leads him up her stairs
the house shudders to warm them
from a wind that has mastered the disjoints;
and the new young vines reach and tremble.
They've come no closer to understanding
the bevels and warps of each other's body,
but had their reflective moments of respite
in the curve of the collarbone,
the jut of narrow hip, deep in solitary sensation—
where why as a word
is finally only a grandmother's whisper.

Naked,
cradling a glass of water,
she faces the sea.
She has slipped down to the window
chilled and wary
for what seemed like thirst,
but she sees now
is so much more
than roses.

Living at the Level of the Spectacular

On the move, it's a rain forest tangled mire,
a desert vast and dry.
It's a river too swift for passage, yet we cross:
we dare to live at the level of the spectacular
searching for truth not sensation
searching for the untouched, unhindered,
unbound and wild brained we search for
one moment at once earth and ourselves
pure, alone, spectacular co-mingling,
it comes from the highest mountain,
the oldest stone, the deepest lake-bed,
it comes from the untamed and the untamable
that furred or feathered guide still fearless,
still spectacular in his wisdom.
Living at the level of the spectacular is bigger
than you and I, it is the moment between breaths—
pure air, pure fire, explosive inspiration
undeniable, unbiddable.
You can't hope for this, it comes of its own,
you can't pray for this— it is no prophesy, it is
an elusive illusory moment: your sad mortal heart
will break apart and leave behind one tiny kernel of grace
as clear as a crystal, the smallest single moment
of remembering beyond yourself,
remembering a once pure
spectacular life from thousands of years ago,
that life a single seed on fire
kindling one spectacular heart.

The Caller

I am an omen, a portent, a sinister
left handed caller from the northland.
I am the bringer of darkness and shedder of light.
I speak in a shadow language ancient tongue
learned at the fire of the stone people long long ago.

I am the reader of the sky, the text of stars lives in me.
I am the one who draws down the moon, casts
her light this way and that, I am truth
and lies, great and small,
full and empty.

My belly has been fecund and it has been wild.
I am the mother and the crone, my dues are paid.
I am the voice you will not hear
the mask you do not see. I am the tongue
that flickers,

the dark cat pacing, the bright eagle soaring.
I am the hummingbird finished with her journey.
Follow me only if you are ready to see the end.
I am the blackness of a day darkened by eclipse,
a volcano erupting. I am the light you cannot see.

I am witch and warrior, caller and called,
eventually you will come to me for answers.
I am searing and shivering, ravaged and blessed,
blind and full with The Sight. A wind lashing, I am fragile
and proud, and I am as old as the mountain you sleep beneath.

I am the Caller, you are the called. In the end
you must ask the questions that need asking,
hear the answers you cannot bear to hear:
the secrets that will break your heart
and leave you wandering, leave you to start again.

I am the Caller and the Called, asked, answered,
howling in the winter wind. Earth shattered. Torn.

Credits

Irish poet Jo Slade inspired the first line of *Black Swan/Eala Dubh* as well as the last line of *Old Lessons* with her beautiful poem *Instruments of Measurement* (from *The Vigilant One*, Salmon Poetry).

The Winter Queen borrows from the lines "I have swallowed a secret burning thread" from the Suzanne Vega song *The Queen and the Soldier*.

Poems on pages 49-68 in Part I were written to pastel images by Julie Higgins. Julie Higgins' work is widely admired and collected. Information about gallery showings and works in progress can be found on her website, www.artistjuliehiggins.com. It was an honor and a pleasure to collaborate with her.

Line credits:
"little cat feet" – from *The Fog*, Carl Sandburg
"Bride of Quiet" – from *Ode on a Grecian Urn*, John Keats
"Abu Ben Adhem, may his tribe increase" – from *Abu Ben Adhem*, James Leigh Hunt
"I come from the place of the Black Sisters and I bring news of war and extinction." - *The Aeneid*, Virgil. Book VII.

Poiêsis Press chose Minion Pro as its house font because it has all of the qualities we aspire to in our publishing: elegance, and an old world quality not overwhelmed but enhanced by a touch of simplicity. We like the direct descenders, the graceful old world g's and a's, the very slight emphasis on elegant serifs for special occasions, but most of all we like its readability. Minion Pro was designed by Robert Slimbach for the Adobe Originals collection, inspired by the typefaces of the late Renaissance.

Jane Galer holds a BA in philosophy, an MA in material culture studies, and a certificate in museum curation for archaeologists. She trained as a shaman in the lineage of the Q'ero of Peru. Her work includes *Becoming Hummingbird: Charting Your Life Journey the Shaman's Way*, *The Navigator's Wife*, a novel, and she is currently at work on *The Painted People: the Celtic Shaman's Lineage*. Jane lives in northern California with her family.

CPSIA information can be obtained at www.ICGtesting.com
Printed in the USA
LVOW07s0928050216

473647LV00005B/36/P